Half-Breed

Hushkachin

PAGE PUBLISHING
Conneaut Lake, PA

First originally published by Page Publishing 2023

ISBN 979-8-88793-869-1 (pbk)
ISBN 979-8-88793-870-7 (digital)

Printed in the United States of America

I dedicate this book to my parents:

John Bahe Nez Hushkashin (06/22/1910–06/16/2004)
Phoebe Betty Yazzie (03/20/1917–09/01/2009)
Harold Dean Cloward (12/29/1921–05/11/2007)
Stella Ruth Young (02/07/1923–10/13/2003)

It was not a chance happenstance that I had four exquisite souls that took interest in me and attended to my basic necessities. They nurtured me away from the venomous values, they fed me when I was hungry for knowledge, and they sheltered me with steel trust in God. I yearn that their time was not spent on me in vain for they loved me unconditionally. I am forever grateful and obligated to my fathers and my mothers. I wrote this book as a tribute to them.

John & Phoebe Nez

Dean & Ruth Cloward

My loving Parents

Acknowledgment

I would like to express my special thanks to my sister, Kathrine Whittekiend, for editing my writing.

Prologue

The title of my book is *Half-Breed*. This title was made known to me years ago. I thought at first it was a comparison of the two cultures in which I grew up, coming from the Navajo Indian Reservation and learning about the outside world. But it turns out that we are all half-breeds, half-human beings and half-spiritual beings. I began writing this book once before, but I was taking a negative approach. My computer crashed, and I lost everything. I then realized it is not about me; it is about all of us.

Introduction

My name is Jerry F. Nez Sr. I am a full-blooded Native American from the Navajo Nation. My clans are Tsinnijinnie (black streak in the wood or forest people) and Tabaha' (Edgewater clan), my grandfather's clan on my mother's side is Tachinid (red running into the water), and my grandfather's clan on my father's side is Tse'njikini (honey-combed rock people). This is how I would formally introduce myself. The Navajo people are a matrilineal and matrilocal society, with each person belonging to four different key clans. The first clan is from the mother, the second is from the father, the third is from the maternal grandfather, and the fourth is from the paternal grandfather. There are many clans, and because the Navajo tribe did not have a written language, the clan system can be very complicated and confusing. The most important thing is to remember who is in your circle of clans. These are the individuals that are most closely related to you; therefore, these are the clan individuals that you can't marry.

This book is an account of some of my experiences and memories. All that I have written is true, but I have left out the names of individuals for privacy reasons. As I remember, some events may become clouded with time, as all things seem to do, similar to a sandstorm covering up footprints.

WOLTA'II

Chapter 1

Family and Early Life

I will begin my story as a young boy on the Navajo Indian Reservation in Arizona, USA. I never grasped the idea of a government controlling a multitude of people against their will, enough control to relocate them to a piece of land called the reservation. It seems improbable here in the land of freedom. I wondered, how can a government comprised of individuals coming from different worlds with diverse cultures, ideals, values, and religious ideologies know what is beneficial for the tribes? Nevertheless, it is my homeland, and I love it.

The landscape is magnificent and is well-known for its scenic beauty. Monument Valley, Shiprock, Window Rock, and Canyon de Chelly are just a few of the distinguished landmarks in my homeland.

I was born in a hogan in the fall of 1953. While my mother was giving birth to me, my uncle, a medicine man, was chanting the good way songs. My mother was in a kneeling position, clinging to a rope that was wrapped around her armpits and secured through an opening in the ceiling. Since there was no analgesic available to help numb the pain, she had a piece of cedarwood placed in her mouth to bite on as the pain became intense. Years later, as a young toddler, I would ask my mother questions about my birth, like how many pounds I was and what time I was born.

She would reply, "You weighed about as much as a small bag of potatoes, and you were born when the sun was high in the sky." We had no measurable devices like they had in the hospitals. Basically, there were no written records about my birth, only word of mouth from my mother and, of course, my body as proof that I happened.

I had tremendous parents who were loving and caring. My father was a passionate physical worker. He was built lean and rugged to match the environment. He was a walking sinew. He did not have any formal schooling in the English language or customs and spoke only his native Navajo dialect. He said to me once, "God made a Navajo, and he gave me words to speak in Navajo. If he wanted me to be someone else, then I would not be me, and if he wanted me to be somewhere else, then I would not be here." He was a stern man yet loved to laugh, especially at his own jokes; he walked as if he were enjoying every step.

My father built our hogan (dwelling) without a measuring tape. I recall watching him shape the cedar logs that he had chopped down and transported by horse and wagon with an ax. He would begin working on the hogan at sunrise and continue until sunset, stopping only for a meal and liquids and never complaining. He would sing medicine songs under his breath and occasionally whistle softly. He made quite an impression on me during my childhood. He taught me not to be lazy and to wake up before sunrise, pray always, speak the truth, and love all things, especially my family.

My mother was the sweetest, kindest, and smartest woman I ever knew. All you had to do was look into her eyes and feel the warm spirit that was inside. She could tell if you were hungry, tired, or sad in an instant, and she would have the cure. She would feed anyone that came into our meek home, whether they were on horseback or driving a fancy truck. Sometimes it would be a cup of warm tea with tortillas if that's all she had to offer. She was well respected among the people. Like my father, she was a hard worker. I remember her bringing a newborn lamb into the hogan and laying it next to the wood stove because it would've frozen if it had been left outside in the winter blizzard. She was proficient in weaving rugs, and it was beneficial for my parent's income.

Her mother passed away when she was attending eighth grade in New Mexico. My grandfather then brought her back at the age of fourteen to raise her younger brother and sister. My grandfather had two wives, and with my grandmother gone, he stayed with his first wife and left my mother and her siblings to forage for themselves by weaving rugs, reproducing her mother's patterns. Each design signified a story or symbol of our culture. She would tell us stories of how hard life was without food, shelter, and water.

Her belief and faith in overcoming any obstacle were extraordinary. She displayed her determination by channeling her wisdom and patience into everyday tasks. She was bigger than life in my eyes. She was the pillar of our clan.

Altogether there were ten children of my parents that my mother gave birth to, but unfortunately, only eight survived. Two girls passed on before I was born. I asked my mother about them a few times, but I could see the sadness in her eyes as her thoughts would go back to a solemn time; hence, I never asked about them again.

I am third from the youngest. Having a life in a remote area where we seldom had any connections with other people, we relied on one another for work, play, and entertainment. We seldom fought among ourselves because we were not only family but also friends. If we got annoyed with one another, there was no one else to associate with.

During my childhood, we lived in a hogan. A traditional hogan is a single-dwelling home usually made either in an octagonal or round shape, with the doorway always facing east. The walls were built with cedar logs, by either laying one over another or standing them horizontally. The roof was constructed in a spiral design as each row would taper over the other until it reached a dome closure. An opening was made for the stove pipe to clear. The logs would be covered with dirt and mud to seal the cracks. Overtime the dirt would harden and almost become water-resistant. The floors were dirt, very simple, but efficient. There was no electricity or running water. Our home was warm in the winter and cool in the summer. The hogans were and are also used for various tribal ceremonies. Currently almost all hogans are made of modern materials and as extravagant as the builder's pocketbook.

Growing up, our parents instructed the family about the sacredness of all living things. We were taught that we are connected to all things here on earth and in the heavens. Therefore, we prayed three times a day—before sunrise with white cornmeal, at high noon with corn pollen, and again at sunset with yellow cornmeal. We prayed over our animals, our land, our crops, our health, and our inner peace between head and heart. We prayed for one another and for peace between heaven and earth, a balance to achieve harmony. We ended our prayers with the words "it is all well again" four times, as we would face in all four directions.

Every household in the Navajo society taught their families good principles and standards of living. There was no written language or doctrine to follow. These core beliefs kept the tribe connected even though we were scattered away from each other.

There were always considerable things to do around our home. A great deal of the activities were preparation for the coming winter. When I was a young boy, my father would say, "If you want to be a man, you will have the horses in the corral before sunrise." So I used that philosophy as a measuring stick to begin my day. My father had many horses. I tried to round them up to no avail. The vastness of the terrain was too great for a little boy to find the herd of mustangs in the dark. I grew up loving horses; they are my favorite animal on earth. My mother told me that when my umbilical cord dried and fell off my belly, they buried it in the horse corral, a common tradition that was practiced by the parents. Whatever they felt their child would excel at is where their umbilical cord would be buried, for example, in the cornfields and sheep corrals.

Consequently, mine ended up in the horse corral. It gives me an extra sense of bonding with them, sort of like a horse whisperer.

Horses and mules were our main means of transportation, either on horseback or by wagon. Gathering firewood in a wagon would be an all-day excursion. Chopping wood was hard work. If you had a dull axe, the work became even more difficult and challenging, but my father always seemed to make the job seem effortless. Going home with a full load of wood was very satisfying. While handling the mules as they pulled the wagon, he never pushed them; he would let them set their own pace.

Getting water from a hand pump well in a wagon was just as demanding—more so for the mules. That is why every cup of water was valuable and appreciated once it was delivered to the hogan.

My parents always grew a variety of corn, squash, and watermelon every spring; it was a family affair. If you were old enough to carry a can of seeds, then you were a farmer. We relied on the rain to water the plants; it was an act of faith. We planted according to the phase of the moon. My father would say, "Sometimes we plant early, sometimes later. When we plant, the moon will give us enough time for the plants to mature and be harvested." It seemed that every year, we would harvest much—enough to share with extended families and friends.

At an early age, I spent the majority of my days herding sheep, most of the time with two of my brothers. My family would turn out the herd from the sheep corral in the early mornings before it got hot. They would herd them toward the wash that was about five miles away. Our mother would feed us prior to beginning our walk. We would gather around a wooden table that elevated a few inches above the dirt floor. Breakfast usually consisted of fresh tortillas, mutton, and potatoes that were served in a big round cast iron skillet. We folded the tortillas to scoop the food since we didn't have enough utensils for everyone. We sipped a cup of hot herbal tea or coffee to go along with our meal. Our parents would make sure before leaving that we each had a water bottle since the high desert heat would sometimes be unforgiving.

My brothers and I would pack a leather sling and a bag of round stones that we would use if we came across any small game. Opposite the sling, we had a handmade slingshot for close-range shooting.

Every day was an adventure as we walked behind the herd to the watering hole. We would easily get distracted but never enough to forget our main objective, which was to get the flock to the wash where the water ran year around. I would wonder why we had to walk when we had so many horses.

In the summertime, we would move to our summer camp because it was closer to the wash than our hogan. Our temporary arraignment for lodging was constructed with scrap lumber, and the roof was comprised of anything available such as old car hoods or corrugated sheet metal. The cooking area was built with cedar poles secured with baling wire. The sleeping quarters for the boys was a government-issued twin bed that my aunt brought from the boarding school where she worked. My father sawed the bed in half, but we lost one half, so I shared the bed with my brother, who is ten years older than me. My other two brothers would sleep on the dirt floor with sheep skin as their mattress and a wool blanket that my mother had woven. My sisters slept in the cooking area with my parents on the dirt floor as well.

I recall an incident I had there at the summer camp. All of my family went away to a ceremony for a couple of days, and I was left alone to tend to the sheep and livestock. This was a tall order for me for I was around seven years of age. Riding a mare bareback, since I was too small to saddle her, I managed to get the flock watered. I hobbled the horse so I could find her easily the next day and retired to the shanty. I ate the supper that my mother made and left for me, consisting of tortillas, dried mutton, and water. I lay down early because I didn't know how to light the kerosene lantern or the oil lamp; besides, there was a full moon that night. I became restless, and I decided that I could use some company so I walked to the sheep corral. I located the largest sheep in the herd which was a wether, a castrated male sheep. He was a tame creature, and his wool was very soft. He let me cuddle up to him. I had just dozed off when there was a loud barking coming from our sheepdogs. There are different kinds of barking, and I recognized that the barking I was hearing was a protective, aggressive one. I stood up and noticed a black figure outside the corral. It was motionless, and the outline was unrecognizable to me. I climbed over the railing and walked slowly toward the creature. The moon was exceptionally bright, but I could not see what this thing was. The dogs were in a frenzy.

As they kicked up dust, they were snarling with their ears pinned back, and the hairs on their backs were standing up. By now, I had edged my way to within six feet of the being. It was totally black, and I noticed it had pointed ears on top of its head. I summoned courage by saying a prayer to the almighty God for protection. I knew that my responsibility was to guard the flock. I had no weapon, just my will. We stood motionless for an infinite time face to face. Finally, the beast shifted and lowered its head. I realized to my relief that it was a horse! It had wandered off from the herd. I crawled back over the fence and nestled against my big comrade, the wether, and fell asleep.

I wonder to myself now and then how much strength it takes for each of us to confront our fears. Maybe we just let ourselves slither away, hoping that it will all go away magically, never realizing that we all have within us the ability to create our own presence by overcoming obstacles that challenge our lives. It takes courage to face uncertainties. In order to eliminate fears, we must have a clear vision of our aspirations and a distinct purpose, energized with intense desire and passion. Fear is an illusion. However powerful it becomes, that is determined by our mind's eye.

One day, I witnessed a conversation between my father and one of my older brothers about a horse that he admired, and my brother asked if he could have it. My father granted the request without much pause, which struck me as odd since this particular brother hardly rode horses or had an interest in doing any chores that had to do with the herd. Later I met with my father and asked him if I could have a horse too. He said, "Your brother is eighteen, and you are only ten, but if you can answer this question, then I will give you a horse. How do you own a living thing?"

I said, "I can't answer that question. I'm too young to know that sort of stuff."

He confidently said, "Exactly! Until you can grasp that concept, then we keep things as they are for now."

A few weeks went by, and I came up with another request for my father about owning a horse. I said, "My father, all of our mares have foaled except for one. The big roan broodmare is the only one left. If I can tell you the color of the colt inside her, can it be mine?"

He paused a moment, and with a slight grin, he said, "The majority of our herd is red roan, so it would not be difficult to predict a roan color, so that color is out. What do you say?"

I said, "Black!"

He was startled and replied, "We have no black studs around this part of the country, and we have no black horses in our herd. So if the mare has a black colt, then it can be yours."

Each day for the next two weeks, I followed that particular family of mustangs, which consisted of eight strong siblings and a mule. Finally, one spring morning, as I was tracking the mare, my father rode up behind me on a horse and asked if I needed a ride. He said, "You left before we had breakfast, so your mother asked me to look for you."

Without any discussion, I blurted out, "I think she had her colt!" I pointed at the mare that was standing with her head down in the tall grass. We approached cautiously so as not to excite her and waited patiently until at last we saw a black stud colt stagger to his feet! He was muscular and athletic. In my excitement, I almost forgot to ask my father, "So, is that my colt?"

My father didn't answer verbally; he just nodded his head and stared at me for a moment as if to wonder, *Who is this kid?*

As the weeks went by, I checked on the colt daily. I didn't give him a name as in our culture we didn't give names to animals except for their physical description. In this case, it was the little black stud. My father discouraged me from bothering the little black stud's family. One day, when my father went away to look for a lost cow, I talked my brothers into helping me saddle up one of the stud horses so that I could go check on the colt. Normally we don't ride with a saddle, but this particular horse was a little green or skittish.

I rode toward Star Mountain, which was located west of our home. Even though my father had many horses, they all grazed apart in little bands, so each meadow had remnants of the herd. As I rode on top of a mesa, I could see the little black stud jumping around his mother and playing with his brothers in a ravine. As I rode closer, I could tell that the stud horse that I was riding was not welcome by the way each of the horses laid their ears back and lowered their heads. I could feel the energy from the horse I was on, who had four sox and a blazed face; he knew that the colt wasn't his. He began dancing and doing some fancy crow hops. I pulled hard on the reins, but he ignored me. I kicked him to get him to turn around, but he was fixed on the little colt. He reared up and began bucking. I knew as long as I was in the saddle that he was unable to get to him, so I held on for all I was worth, which didn't amount to much at that point in my life. I might have weighed sixty pounds soaking wet. I stayed on until the saddle got loose, and it flipped under his belly. All I could see were hooves flying and stirrups snapping as I hit the dirt! I looked up to see the stud race toward the colt that was being protected by his mother. The brothers, along with the mule, made a sturdy wall. The stud took some hellacious hits as he made his way to the colt. I saw him try to stomp on the little colt, but the mother bumped him off his mark and gave him numerous bites. The stud was determined; he overcame countless kicks as he located the colt again in the chaos. He bit the colt on the neck and picked him up like a rag doll. He shook him back and forth until he ripped the hide off. I couldn't watch any longer; I grabbed a branch off a sagebrush and went into the fracas. I figured if I could hit the stud across his nose, which is a tender spot, I might be able to slow his attack. I ran in between animals weighing thousands of pounds that were swiftly clashing, dust was flying, and the sounds that came out of these creatures were bizarre. It was a mixture of outlandish bloodcurdling, snorting, and shrieking cries. The last thing I remember was taking a swing with the sagebrush branch. Then there was silence, total stillness.

I lay there, examining my body with my eyes closed. I felt a sharp pain in the back of my head. I asked myself what happened as I began moving my toes, then my fingers. Thank goodness, my body was intact! I opened my eyes to see that I was alone. The dust had settled, mostly on my clothes. I staggered up, and balancing myself upright, I slowly walked from the ravine and looked around for any sign of life that resembled horses. Gradually my eyes cleared up from the grime, and as I stood there surveying the landscape, I noticed a slight sign of movement way off in the distance. The horses were racing wildly, and I assumed the stud was still creating havoc and the little black stud had survived the initial attacks. I knew there was nothing I could do, so I began making my way home.

The sun was high and scorching, and I was getting thirsty by the time I walked into the hogan. My mother was inside and looked at me with bewilderment as she asked if I was okay. I said I was fine, but she asked again what had happened. I said I got bucked off, too afraid to tell her the whole story. She said, "Take your shirt off," and she gently helped me remove my T-shirt. She showed me the dry blood stain that had saturated the back of the shirt. She washed my head in the wash basin and noticed that I had suffered deep lacerations. If we had lived near a hospital, I would have received multiple stitches, but we had no means of travel to get treatment, so my mother applied juniper sap to the wound and wrapped my head with a cloth. I was as good as new. However, when my father returned shortly after his ride, he became upset at the news of what had happened to me. I don't know if it was because of my injury or losing a saddle. He left immediately, knowing there wasn't much daylight left. My father had few words to say, no matter the situation. If he did speak, it was plain and straightforward; his action always spoke louder. As evening approached, I could hear the sounds of hooves and the dogs barking; it was a signal that something was approaching. I ran and opened the horse corral in time for my father to lead the stud through the gate. He had roped him and towed him back. I was sorry to see the saddle was missing and the reins and bit were trashed. I couldn't find the words to apologize for the remorse I felt. My father knew my feelings. He put his hand on my shoulder as we walked back to our hogan. He let me know that the little black stud colt was alive and well.

The next day, he castrated the stud. My father said, "A wild stud causes chaos and will scatter your herd. Raging testosterone in any creature is unhealthy and will be destructive."

I realized then the wisdom behind the question that my father asked me, "How do you own a living thing?" When we claim anything to be ours, it is really a deceptive statement because we do not have the capability or the power to regulate any other thing that is a living entity. We can only be a steward, not a possessor. I recall one occasion when my father had just ridden horseback from a funeral. While he was still mounted on his horse, he said, "I just came back from a burial rite for a man who when alive said he owned all this land." He motioned with his arm from one horizon to the other. "So I was curious to see how much land he really owned when they buried him, and all he needed was about three feet by eight feet." Having learned a valuable lesson about the ownership of living things, I decided that the little stud colt was a friend. Of course, this was only in my mind. I didn't ask what the little black colt thought.

Chapter 2

Education

When I turned six years old, I went through a formality that occurred throughout the reservation every fall. It was to be recruited by the Bureau of Indian Affairs, or BIA, for the boarding schools. The government established these schools on or near the reservations to provide an education for children that lived in remote locations, and that was about 99 percent of the population. At that age, I had no way of knowing what I was in for when my mother sat me down and tried to explain to me why I needed to go away to school. She said that I would learn to read, write, count, and even speak the White man's language. She said, "It will be good for you and our people."

The day came to begin our journey to the boarding school. My father hitched the mules to the covered wagon. An arch was made from hardwood that curved in a "U" shape and was fastened into a metal bracket on the side of the bed. A canvas was draped snuggly around these "ribs" and also fastened to the sides of the wagon. My mother put a mattress and sheep hide inside to give it a cozy warm feeling. My father had a barrel of water attached to one side of the wagon for us and the mules to drink. My mother packed provisions to eat like boiled mutton, corn, flour, and coffee. It would be an all-day trek over dirt roads that were seldom traveled. It was a slow journey. Sometimes, when I got bored, I would run beside the wagon or stop and look at the scenery since this was the first time I had ever left our basin.

As the sun began to set and we arrived near the boarding school, my father pulled the wagon under a big cottonwood tree and unhitched the mules, let them graze, and gave them water. My mother started a fire and began cooking supper. I looked at the buildings across the wash, wondering what all the bright lights symbolized, but I was still more captivated by the lights from the moon and stars. As I gazed into the night, listening to the crickets chirping, I fell asleep.

The next morning, we had a quick breakfast from the leftovers. My mother walked me to Seba Dalkia Boarding School, a school that was constructed on the Navajo Indian Reservation in the 1950s by the Bureau of Indian Affairs (BIA) for educating youths between the ages of six and eight years old. As we stepped into the spacious building with large windows, we were greeted by a female Navajo staff employee. She spoke in our native language, "Ya'at'ee'h," which means hello and also could mean good, depending on the situation. The proper response back then would be to repeat "Ya'at'ee'h." If the parties knew each other's clan, then they would insert that into the introduction with a soft handshake; a smile would cement the greetings. Since we were there specifically for business, all the small talks were bypassed. She sat down at a desk, pulled out a form, and began asking questions about me such as what my name was.

My mother answered "Jerry," but my mother called me "As kee li baha" (the light-colored one).

Then came another question, "When was he born?"

My mother replied, "In the fall."

When the lady said, "I need a specific date."

My mother responded, "Around the time they eat turkeys."

The worker said, "Okay we will put his date of birth as Thanksgiving Day," and so it was from that day in the BIA records I was officially born on November 25, 1953. There were no records of my birth from the medicine man who delivered me since we had no formal writings.

After we had completed all the questions, it was time for my mother to leave. It was a moment in time that I recall clearly because of the feeling of desolation. I've always had my mother's love and strength to comfort me. Now, at such a young age, I was thrust into a state of autonomy. I looked around to see if anyone could see my alligator tears forming, and then I quickly realized that there were many boys and girls that were in the same situation as myself. I stood up bravely and transformed into a little big man. My mother gave me a passionate hug that would last me for the remainder of the school year. I watched her until she blended in with the trees and brush. I held onto a paper sack that contained a few clothing items that my mother had packed for me. It wasn't enough to get me through the week, let alone the next nine months. I began my journey into the abyss of rules and regulations that were enforced with stern discipline by the BIA boarding school staff. Looking back, I would best describe it as a boot camp for children between six and eight years old. I underwent a physical makeover. It began with taking a shower with a dozen other boys, sharing eight shower heads in front of a stern-looking female assistant. We were required to lather our bodies from head to toe. Those who had the most suds were picked to rinse and leave, and the rest had to keep layering soap until they were dismissed from the showers. Next, I received a haircut that was so short that my head looked blue. I then received my government-issued clothes, which I put into my assigned locker. Later, I got my vaccinations. Afterward I met a dentist. It turned out to go well since I had not been exposed to a lot of artificial sweeteners in my diet.

Over the next few weeks, we were constantly reminded to not speak our native tongue, Navajo, and to begin speaking English. If you control people's words, you control their thoughts, and because we didn't know how to utter sentences in English, the dormitory became a muted subdued asylum. Once we were away from the staff, we would speak Navajo covertly.

When it was time to eat, we gathered in a single file in the cafeteria, alternating with the girls. There were tables set up in a neat order, and the seats were attached to the tables. It would be the first time I would eat on a tile floor.

We stood with attentiveness, not speaking. We were not allowed to be spirited, and after receiving our grub, we surrounded the table and waited until the last person filled the last empty spot. Then we would all sit down in unison. We had to eat in a clockwise pattern, saving the dessert until the last. If we slouched while eating, we would receive a smack on our backs with a yardstick. We would get a blow to our fingers if we scraped our plates. We were not allowed to leave until everyone had cleaned their plates, so when we were all done with our meals, we would signal the staff member by raising our hands. A staff member would then inspect our plates before giving consent for us to exit in an orderly fashion. This would be our daily ritual each time we ate in the cafeteria henceforth.

I recall one incident when all the boys around the table wanted to leave quickly because there were just a few bicycles available on a first-come-first-serve basis. That meant we had to beat the other tables out the door, but we had twin girls at our table. They were a little spindly and would not eat their food. We tried to urge them to eat without drawing attention to ourselves but realized it was futile to expect the girls to devour their meal. So we devised a plan to help the girls clean off their plates. Every time the staff member left our table, we would rotate our plates to the right, and whoever acquired the plate with the food would try to gulp it down. If he was full, then he would stuff the remaining grub into his pockets. After a couple of rotations, all the plates were ready for inspection, and off we went onto the playgrounds.

Dormitory life was quite an adjustment for me. At night, I missed my warm, soft wool mattress and blankets; the cold sheets never replaced that sensation of comfort. The glimmer of the moon and stars were obscured by the hallway lights, and the cozy flickering woodstove was replaced by a hot water radiator system that clanked all night.

All activities were done as a unit, from getting up in the mornings to going to bed at night. I thought to myself, *Now I know how sheep must feel.* It was difficult for me since I was accustomed to being a loner and doing things at my own pace, without being confined by fences.

I recollect one time when all our chores were completed and we had playtime. The boys wanted me to play a game with them. I refused to participate and sat against an old stone building, just content to relax and watch the kids amuse themselves. As I began daydreaming about my home, I was interrupted again by the boys asking if I could play with them; they said they just needed one more to even out the numbers. I asked them what they were playing. They said cowboys and Indians. I told them that I was not going to be a cowboy. I'd be an Indian, not just any Indian, but the chief. They all agreed, and I became the dominant ruler of my twenty-member clan. The cowboys had made a fort out of tumbleweeds down in a wash, and we were supposed to run in circles while they shot at us like in the movies. I devised a war strategy that would have made Chief Joseph proud. I told them we would not be running in circles around the fort with bows and arrows made out of sagebrush branches while we got shot at. I divided the band into two parties. The first group would cut clubs from the nearby cedar trees, then hide on the getaway path, and wait for my signal to attack. The second group dug eight-inch-diameter holes about a foot deep, put twigs across the lairs and covered them with paper, and sprinkled sand to finish the traps on the escape route side of the fort. I took a little combatant with me, and we crawled outside the property zone, the forbidden barrier that was marked by the BIA workers with red paint on the electrical poles. I knew that we would not be spotted since everyone obeyed the rules. We snuck and inched next to the tumbleweed fort. I could hear the cowboys laughing and having a good time. The next act is something I am not proud of, but at a young age, I was convinced we were in a real battle and this feat was a military action. The reason I had taken a partner was that he had some matches! I lit the fort! The fire shot straight up, and the cowboys tore down the fort so fast that they began scampering toward the snares. I then signaled for my first group to attack with their imaginary bows and arrows. I don't know what the Battle of Little Big Horn was like, but I think I was close to recreating it with the chaos that was materializing in front of me! There was smoke bellowing, dust flying, and a battlefield full of wounded cowboys. Just as we were rounding up the last of the cowboys as our prisoners, we heard the fire siren, and two BIA trucks skidded to a stop. The staff rushed down to extinguish the remaining residue of the fort. We were all rounded up in a single file and made to stand at attention while we were interrogated. Not one single warrior would disclose my plot, and they were all ready to take the punishment for what happened. But I could not let that happen, so I stepped forward and declared myself the main outlaw of the renegades. As it turned out, three of us were found guilty as charged and condemned to a lashing with a two-inch leather strap and one week of no supper, no playtime, and hard labor, which consisted of mopping the bathroom and hallways.

The first couple of days of the punishment went routine, but on the third night, I was awoken by someone shaking my arm. I realized it was my little combatant with whom I was sentenced. I asked, "What's up?"

He said, "I'm really hungry."

So I said, "Okay, let's get you something to eat." I quietly rolled out of the top bunk bed and crawled on my hands and knees with my little friend right behind me. We made it to the end of the barracks, then quickly passed the corridor where the staff members would frequently pass as they tended to their duties. Off we went into the cafeteria and the pantry. I closed the door and turned on the lights, and to our amazement, we beheld countless assortments of provisions on the shelves. We were in a gold mine to satisfy starving kids. I asked proudly, "What would you like to eat?" And my little pal pointed to a half-gallon metal container of sliced peaches. I said, "Okay," and began opening it with a can opener. When I removed the lid, my little buddy reached in and began gorging himself until he couldn't stuff anymore into his belly. We made our way back, concealing our tracks and silently creeping into our beds. The next morning, we woke up normally to the voice of the staff member and the glaring bright fluorescent lights. We made our beds swiftly to pass inspection, grabbed our school clothes, and headed to the showers. By the time we were ready for breakfast, the staff members were alerted to an incident in the kitchen—a forced entry in the pantry and a possible felony, since it happened on federal property. An investigation was launched as we ate, all heads turned like swiveling toys. My little friend looked scared, and I nodded my head sideways to say, "Don't volunteer any material or testimony." As it turns out, we left enough evidence from the peaches on our hands that led right to our beds. My friend and I were rounded up and confronted with the proof. I didn't want to challenge their findings; I knew it was pointless. I pleaded that my little comrade was famished, that it was heartless and cruel to make him go without food, and that it was my idea to get some nourishment from the kitchen. The judgment and sentence were passed quickly by the staff. Our punishment was getting whipped again with the leather strap. However, we were allowed to eat supper for the remainder of our time, which lasted another week. I don't know what happened to my little sidekick after that; I think he might have realized that it was a good idea that he kept his distance from me.

I came to the realization after this ordeal that I couldn't be the free spirit that I was and I had to conform to different values and ideas. Instead of hearing echoes of horse hooves, I heard the shuffling of shoes in the hallways; instead of hearing the animals proclaim a new dawn with their own expressions, I heard the staff members bellowing out a racket that blasted the peaceful sunrise away. The presence of my mother's soft hands and sweet voice was replaced by cold-blooded, unkind, and cruel beings. Needless to say, I was never asked to play in any reindeer games again.

Speaking of reindeer, my first introduction to the Christmas holiday was bizarre, mainly because I had never heard of Christmas, Jesus Christ, or the Bible. My family had their own faith and creed. So when I heard from the staff personnel that Santa was coming soon with his reindeers, I took notice. I wanted to see this Santa, and to my amazement, when I saw a poster hanging in the hallway of Santa Claus, I thought to myself that there was no way a human being could look like this picture. I studied the poster of a White man with red cheeks, a white beard, a red outfit, and a floppy hat. Up to that point, I had seen less than five White men and women. These were comprised of the trading post owners and the principal and his wife at the boarding school. I wondered, how can adults believe in such madness? Furthermore, the staff personnel cut down a perfect spruce tree and brought it inside the building, where they strung lights all over the sapling. I questioned this behavior—couldn't they see that we as humans cannot possibly enhance the beauty of nature? This tree will shrivel up and die once it has been cut off from its roots like all organic structures. I was told that Santa Claus would put presents under the tree for all good boys and girls.

As the time grew closer to Christmas Day, I saw all the different denominations competing to enroll the children into their memberships so the kids would get gifts from their institutions. My friends encouraged one another to join as many churches as possible before Christmas so as to benefit from the numbers when it came to getting candies and gifts.

One day, I recall the kids getting all excited about "Father." They were dancing jovially and declaring, "Father is here! Father is here!" I wondered if my father was really here. I ran to the window looking for my father, and I saw this White man climbing out of a car dressed in a brown robe with a cross hanging from his neck. He was smiling and shaking the children's hands. He then gave each kid a sack full of candies and nuts. I stood and watched, perplexed at the sight, when one of the staff members asked me why I didn't go get a bag of candy.

All I remember saying was "He's not my father."

Finally, Christmas morning arrived. The staff woke us up by saying, "Wake up! Santa came last night. He brought you all presents." I was a nonbeliever and was suspicious of this man Santa Claus. How can this person find me when he doesn't even know I exist? We all gathered around the tree, and sure enough, there were lots of presents wrapped in colorful, shiny paper, and each gift had a name tag. We all waited patiently; when a name was called, the child would walk up and receive the gifts and sit down and open the presents. After everyone had been given a gift, there were five of us still standing since our names had not been called out. One of the staff members quickly picked out a gift that read "boy" for the boys and "girl" for the girls. I was handed a box wrapped in red glossy paper. I crawled under a table in the dining area because I didn't want anyone to see me open the box. I was intrigued when a metal airplane appeared; the wings folded down. After examining it, I noticed one of the tires was missing, the cockpit windshield was cracked, and the paint had faded. I thought then that I had known there was something distrustful about this man Santa, with his beady little eyes. Nevertheless, it was my first toy that wasn't made with clay. I edged my way out from under the table to join the excitement and energy that had begun around the Christmas tree. The children were all smiling and joyful as they played with their new toys. When the clatter quieted down and calmness prevailed, the kids were showing one another their new prizes.

They asked me what I got, and I said, "Airplane." I had left it in the box for fear of being teased since it was missing a tire and had a busted windshield. However, overtime, the word got out, and not too many kids wanted to swap toys with me briefly just to see who had the coolest toy.

Life is always a teacher of wisdom, and time reveals all things. At the end of the school year, all the plastic, shiny toys were scraped, broken, and lost. Yet, I still had my metal airplane, still in the same condition as it was when I opened it on Christmas Day. It became a popular item to barter for candy and other precious goods in exchange for short-term flights.

The BIA dormitory is not a place for rearing youth. It lacks the affection of family members. There's an absence of edification from the staff personnel. On the contrary, we were subjugated into a White culture and punished for being a Navajo. We were chastised for speaking our native tongue. The ideals that were instilled and demonstrated through ceremonies to us by our fathers and mothers were removed by constant admonishments. On the other hand, I also understand the need for education. We cannot live like our forefathers as the rest of the world is walking on the moon. Each individual must find a balance, a harmony, in keeping their heritage and customs without neglecting the necessity of an education. Our minds ought to be open to new ideas and technology without surrendering our identity. In order to soar like an eagle, we must first gain strength from the nutrients given to us while we are still fledglings in the nest.

In the spring, the day came to go back home. The school year had ended, and the summer vacation arrived not too soon for me. I had just completed my third-grade education, which was the highest grade obtainable at the Seba Dalkia Boarding School. I would not return again to the place that my mother said was a place for learning the White man's language and teachings. I did manage, after a struggle, to grasp the basic courses of math and English. It was a challenging task since I couldn't speak the language. Somehow, I managed a passing grade.

WOLTA'II
Chapter 3

A New Beginning

The summer was a time to be free, smell freedom on the back of a horse, and let the breeze blow my cares away. I was as happy as any animal being set free from a cage. I would revisit all the places that I could only dream about as I lay in bed at the dormitory. I savored the time for I knew that each day was precious. Even our chores of tending to the livestock and gathering firewood for the winter were a time spent in pleasure.

In August of that year, after concluding a day of chores, we sat together as a family over hot tea, tortillas, and some lamb meat. We welcomed the cool, dry air of the early evening as we finished our supper and retired for the night. In the high deserts, the twilights were serene and soothing, but the calmness would sometimes be interrupted by the chirping of a cricket or snoring from my brothers. As I stated before, I shared a twin bed with my older brother, who was ten years older, while my other brothers lay on sheepskin and wool blankets on the dirt floor. This evening started out as a typical night, but it would have a profound effect on me for the rest of my life. I had just drifted off to sleep when a bright light gleamed in my eyes. The brightness of the light was astonishing. I elbowed my brother to wake him, but it was ineffective, and I tried to speak but was unable to utter a sound. I noticed the glow was coming from the south side of the house, and beams of light were radiating through the cracks between the boards that made up the walls. I extended my hand into the light to see if it was real, and I noticed the shadow of my hand and arm on the floor. I realized at that moment that the beam of light was tangible. I slowly rose out of bed and crept over my brother. I gripped the frame of the makeshift window, which didn't have glass, just an open space. I stuck out my head, and to my amazement, I saw a living being suspended in the air. I was only a few feet from this entity, so I clearly observed his appearance. I noticed that he was a man, he had no facial hair, the hair on his head was perfectly shaped, and his face was sculpted and chiseled. He wore a white robe that covered his feet. He had a calm, knowing smile, and his eyes were piercing; they looked right through me as if he could see all my experiences since my birth. He spoke to my mind telepathically, saying, "Total intelligence is unconditional love." It was neither in Navajo or English; it was spoken in the language of the soul or life force. At that moment, I looked down at myself and noticed that my body was shaking from the event. I became aware that there were two parts of me—one physical and one spiritual. The physical is weak and defenseless, while the spiritual is strong and powerful.

My body was telling me, "You are eight years old. You are a Navajo. What is happening is abnormal," while the spiritual side was familiar with this personage in past existence. When I reunited my body and spirit, I jumped back into bed, burrowed under my brother, and put my fist over my eyes so as to block out the bright light. After a few moments, I peeked to see if the light was still there and was startled to see the light had turned yellow, a soft, warm light. This time, the light was coming from the east. As I followed it, I saw it was the sun—the beginning of a new day! *How can that be?* I wondered as I told myself that I had just laid down for the night. I crawled out of bed and walked out to the south side of the house, looking for any physical evidence of the encounter. I recall that it was a beautiful morning, and as the birds were chirping, my mother walked up to me and asked what I was doing up so early. I said that I was just enjoying the morning. I was hesitant about letting anyone know what I had experienced that night.

Three days later, my mind was still occupied with the perfect image of the divine being. I thought if I went for a ride on a horse, it would be good therapy. After riding for a couple of miles, I noticed a reflection coming from our sheep camp. Whenever there were urgent messages to be sent, we would use a mirror to redirect the rays of the sun precisely in the direction of the party to be alerted. I promptly rode to camp to see what was happening. The signal was not from a mirror but from a white pickup truck parked next to the place. There were two White boys dressed in white shirts and ties talking with my parents. I thought these boys must be lost and asking for directions. I rode closer to get the gist of the conversation. There was something peculiar about our visitors; they transmitted a peaceful energy that aired righteous personas. Normally my father would chase the kids away while the senior folks visited, but this time, he said, "Let us all hear what they have to say," despite the fact that he could not speak or understand English. We eagerly gathered around the two young men.

One of them said, "We are missionaries from the Church of Jesus Christ of Latter-day Saints. We bring you a message about your ancient grandfathers, who lived on this continent many years ago." He reached into his hand-bag and pulled out a blue book with gold lettering. He continued, "In this book is the writing of your people." My mother would interrupt to translate for my father. My father would nod his head as he comprehended and sig-naled with his hand to continue. The missionary opened the book and turned to a page with a picture of a man whom he declared helped translate the *Book of Mormon*. As I looked to see the portrait of this man named Joseph Smith, I was stunned because his picture was identical to the being that I had seen in my vision!

Without thinking, I blurted out, "I saw this man!" All eyes turned to me, and the room became still. I felt a heavy load of anxiety consume me, and I immediately jumped up and left the meeting. After about a half-hour, I returned, and the discussion had turned to education. The missionaries explained that the church had a program called the Indian Placement Program, where school-age children would live with a foster family for the school year and return to their families in the summer.

My mother became excited and said, "I have been praying for my kids to have a better education. This is the answer to my prayers." She asked the missionaries, "How do we sign him up?" They clarified that I had to be a member of the church. My mother responded, "Well, make him a member."

The missionaries said, "He has to be baptized."

My mother again replied, "Baptize him then." The missionaries then stated that I would have to take lessons. My mother answered, "Give him lessons."

Because the deadline to enroll in the placement program was only a week away, I received a crash course in the teachings, beliefs, and doctrine of the gospel of the Church of Jesus Christ of Latter-day Saints. It was a lot of material for an eight-year-old "Rez boy." Obviously, I did not retain many of the teachings, but the missionaries did follow the guidelines, and in less than a week, I was baptized in the Holbrook Arizona Stake House. I did not understand all that was taking place, but I trusted my mother for she was a noblewoman in my eyes. I believed in and respected her counseling. She would say, "Every now and then, you must take risks in order to move ahead." I figured I must be similar to the Mars probe in order to survey and discover what is out there for myself.

A couple of days after my baptism, it was time for me to board the Continental Trailway Bus. Normally, my family would have a ceremony for whoever was leaving for a foreign land, but it was such a short notice that we hardly had any time to prepare. Since my parents were not wealthy as in worldly riches, I hardly had any school clothes to take with me—just the garb that I was wearing and a few items in a paper bag. The missionaries helped us get to the location to meet the bus. It was an intimidating experience. I gave my mother a big hug, a hug that would last me nine months. My father would never say goodbye, so he walked quietly away.

I had no idea where I was headed as I boarded the big bus that was already sputtering black smoke. I found a seat next to a window and tried to get one last glance at my parents. The seat was so big that it felt like I was inside a barrel. Soon the bus was filled with children who were in the placement program. I could hear mixed emotions from the sounds they were making, from laughter to sobbing. For me, I just stared into space as the bus began its trek.

This was the first time I had left the reservation, so I viewed the terrain as we sped past it. The familiar landmarks began vanishing as new shapes appeared. The sun began to set as we continued our journey. My mind would drift to my homeland, wondering what my family was doing, but I knew it was too late to turn back. Besides, the big bus didn't seem to ever get tired.

I began to see the stars appear in the heavens. My father taught us how to scan the constellations as we sometimes had to ride our horses at night. I located the Big Dipper and knew I could find the North Star because the two outermost stars in the bowl pointed to it. The North Star is pretty much fixed in the northern sky, so now I could tell which direction we were traveling. I kept a watchful gaze, but my eyelids started getting heavy sometime in the night, and somewhere along the path I fell asleep.

I woke up in a strange and wonderful place, next to the splendid Wasatch mountains in Utah, USA. The sun was about an hour away from rising, yet I could make out the magnificent mountains that reached beyond the clouds. There was still snow visible on the peaks, but on the foothills, the green grass looked like velvet. The air was humid, so I knew there was plenty of water nearby. I thought that if our livestock could graze on these highlands, they would be heavy animals. My musing was interrupted when a man boarded the bus and asked if we would exit the bus and follow him into a brick building with spacious glass windows. As we walked, I noticed the fine-looking grass that was manicured with precision.

Inside we were met with many volunteers, each carrying items signifying their craft. We began with a shower, then a haircut, and next a dentist. After that, we were given a physical. After that, we went into a room that had clothes and shoes. I received a new pair of black shoes and socks, underwear, shirt and pants, and even a belt. We began like an old chunk of coal and came out like a diamond. We ate a light breakfast, and then we were ready to meet our foster families.

We were escorted into a large room, where we waited for our names to be called out. It was a tense time for me. I was reminded of some events when I was at the boarding school, but this place was more humane, and all the staff had caring smiles and were compassionate. Before long, my name was called out, but I didn't answer. Then my name was repeated again, and again, I didn't answer. The staff began nervously walking around, inspecting all the boys' name tags. Finally, they found me, and with relief in her voice, the helper shouted, "Here he is!" She took me by the hand and led me to a cubical that had my caseworker and my foster mother and sister, Joan. I knew I was being introduced, but with a limited understanding of the English language, it was difficult to answer back. But my foster mother didn't need to hear me respond; she felt with her heart, and she gave me a bear hug as she cried. I looked at my foster sister, Joan, and she also was wiping away tears. I had never seen any grown-up so emotional before; I was a little perplexed, hoping that I didn't do anything wrong. As I came to be familiar with the family, shedding tears was a trademark of theirs. I figured they were manifesting what was in their hearts and squeezing it out through their eyes.

We got into a light green car. I sat in the back seat, and from there, I could see many spacious buildings and congested traffic. I hadn't realized there were so many White people in the world.

The beauty of the land was overtaken by humans' industrious appetite. There were too many roads, but not enough to satisfy the automobiles that cluttered them. I looked to the skies, but the wires hanging from post to post blocked the clouds. I scanned the landscape for animals, but the ones I spotted were all in pens or fenced in; none were free to run. A feeling of being in a foreign land began to swell in the pit of my stomach. I convinced myself that this is a mysterious place, and I wanted to return to my homeland, which I loved, where there are no fences or boundaries and where riches are not measured by time or artificial substances. I devised a plan. I thought, *When these people go to sleep tonight, I will take some of their food and put it in a gunny sack, find some water, and run away.* I planned to travel at night, guided by the stars, and sleep during the day. It took the big bus all night to get here, so I believed I could be home in about two weeks. As I was contemplating my plot, we pulled into the driveway, and my foster mother said, "This is our home." It was a magnificent house compared to our summer sheep camp. As I stepped onto the concrete surface, I encountered another unusual miracle. While standing next to the car, I saw that my foster mother and sister were in a "frozen state." My foster mother was motionless as she was in the act of swinging the car door open, and my foster sister was stationary as she stood next to the car on the driver's side with the keys in her hand. I glanced back and forth and even took a step toward them to get a closer look.

Then suddenly I heard a most powerful, deep voice, a voice so great that when he spoke, the concrete below my feet shook, and I understood that if this almighty being blown on the majestic mountains, they would dissolve into dust. Then I heard him speak; the tone was like a rumbling before thunder. He said, "Trust them. These are good people." Instantly, after hearing these words, everything came alive again. My foster mother and sister did not have a clue what had just happened. As for me, I became conscious of the fact that we are not alone. Furthermore, all my thoughts of running away vanished instantly. I obeyed without question and recognized my foster family as part of my new spiritual family tree. Moreover, they were stuck with me.

I was introduced to the rest of the family, which consisted of three girls and one boy. The oldest, named Lorene, was attending college and had moved out of the house. She is a very kind-hearted, sweet person. Next came Kathrine. She was a tough girl; you didn't want to get on her bad side. She is very bright in terms of textbook learning. Joan is the youngest of the girls. She was nice-looking and looked after me as a big sister. She always had a gentle smile. The one and only boy was Craig. He is a private person, and we grew up tolerating one another. I tried to keep out of his way most of the time, and I felt his relief when it was time for me to return to my natural folks for the summer each year.

My foster mother was a duplicate of my natural mother—a wise, generous, understanding teacher who was always ready to give hugs to anyone. My foster father is the one whose influence I could feel while in his presence. He had an aura that felt like a grizzly bear in sheep's clothing. His shoulders were as broad as the hallway, but his eyes sparkled, and along with his contagious smile, this eased his physical intimidation. Like my natural father, he was a very hard worker and observant of his religious faith. He took me aside the first day and said these words that still resonate with me today: "If you do the following three things, don't lie, don't steal, and don't cheat, we will get along just fine."

In the spring, he had a crew of men from New Zealand that would shear sheep by the thousands in the western states. Then in the early summer and into the fall, he would cut timber in the mountains, stockpile the logs on the property, and saw them into boards. In November and December, he would cut Christmas trees in Colorado by truckload. He sold some to a wholesaler, and the rest he brought to the yard to sell during the holiday season.

My foster parents are the ones that played a significant role in my upbringing and learning. They gave their means and time to see that I had clothes on my back, food in my belly, and shelter from the cold. I am forever grateful to them as well as my natural parents. I struggle each day to not let their work go to waste. I strive to emulate their compassion for those less fortunate than myself. The almighty voice that I heard was right; my foster family were not perfect, but they were good people, and I was safe.

WOLTA'II

Chapter 4

Back to Education (This Time in Utah)

I began my elementary education at the Brockbank School in Spanish Fork, Utah. My foster mother took me to school and enrolled me in the fourth grade. I was introduced in front of the class. I was so petrified inside that I didn't look up at all the white eyes that were examining me. I was seated behind a pretty girl named Vickie. When I looked up, I noticed she had red hair! I'd never seen red hair before, only on cattle and red feathers on chickens. When she wasn't watching, I would rub her hair in amazement. Sometimes, when she moved quickly, my fingers would get stuck in her long locks, and she would just smile. Later, we became friends, and we would play on the sidewalks during recess. I challenged her to a race, and to my disbelief, she beat me! I thought to myself, *How can this be? I was the fastest runner at the boarding school, and this girl is quicker than me?* We kept racing for a couple of weeks until I won. Sometimes I think she just let me win so I would be content. I didn't ask for a rematch. We played other games like marbles and tag.

I learned that her folks had sheep, cattle, and horses too. If she had been a boy, she would have been my best buddy.

Just about two months had gone by when the teacher decided to have a spelling contest where he would take one boy and one girl for a plane ride since he was a pilot. Vickie asked me if I ever rode in a plane. I said never. Then she told me that if I won the spelling contest, I could take my first flight. I replied that I couldn't win, but she said, "You're not stupid. How many in our class can speak two languages? You just have to apply yourself to studying." So we did. All week, we studied during recess, at lunch, and while riding the bus. Finally, Friday arrived, the day for the spelling contest. I scored a perfect 100 percent, and so did Vickie! She was excited, and I thought we would go for a ride in an airplane. But the teacher said that I couldn't have aced the test and that I must have copied Vickie's answers. I was disqualified. In addition, I was taken out of the special education class. I was exposed—no more cookies and no more movies. I thought that was not a scholarly move, but I was taught a valuable lesson—that if you apply your energy and mindset to learning, you can make the impossible possible. Also, on occasion, you can't change the image of yourself to others even if they have the proof in their hands. Vicky was my classmate for only one more year, and after that, we never hooked up as fellow pupils until we graduated from high school. I don't know if she ever realized how important of a mentor and friend she was when I truly needed a helpmate.

There was a curly blond-headed boy named Brad, whom my foster mother asked if he could watch me to make sure that I caught the right bus home. Through the years, Brad and I became close friends, and we spent many years together exploring the terrains of Utah, hunting little critters, and cooking them in our mess kits. I had a hard time at first pronouncing his name between Brad and bread. We went to church together, played basketball, and just hung out. He had lots of brothers who were older than us, but no sisters. Between Brad and Vickie, I was in good hands at the start of my complicated life. It was like I just learned to play football on the reservation with all its rules, and now I am playing basketball in the White man's world with new rules.

My first week at school was full of rough times. My first hurdle was trying to learn to speak English better. I was put into a special education class with some of the slower learners in school for a couple of hours a day. I felt out of place at first until we were treated to cookies and fruits and entertained with movies. Then I thought, *Okay, I can handle this.*

On the second day, the teacher said that I needed to catch up with the class in reading, so he gave me a list of books to study from the library. As I walked down the hallway to the library, I was confronted by a fifth grader who began pushing me around. I tried ignoring him by speeding by him and darting into the library. After the librarian had gathered an armful of books for me to read, I was making my way back to class. The same bully was waiting for me in the hallway. He began pushing me again and knocking my books onto the floor. I studied the boy and thought to myself, If you were at the boarding school, I would've put you on the ground already. But here, I felt immobilized, and besides, I didn't want to get into trouble. I quickly picked up my books and started walking away, and again he bashed them to the floor.

He smirked and said, "What's the matter? Are you a chicken?" Now that's a phrase that was used in the dormitory that I could understand. If you were called out as a chicken, that was a pretty low depiction of your manhood. If you had any spine, you would fight.

So I said with my best English, "After school, I will fight you." And the bully left, and I picked up my books and went back to class, not mentioning a word of what had happened to anyone. When the school bell rang to signal the end of the day, we all scurried in confusion to gather our books and personal belongings. Brad and I headed to the bus, and there was a crowd that had formed a circle, making a commotion. Right in the middle of the ring was the bully from the hall; he was calling me out to fight him.

I asked Brad to hold onto my books, and he said, "You only have two minutes before the bus leaves!"

I said, "I'll make it." I turned to the human circle, and it opened when I entered and closed behind me. I quickly said, "Hurry. Hit me three times. Then I will kill you" (metaphorically speaking, of course). At the boarding school, if you were really a mean tough dude and wanted to show others how brave you were, you would let your opponent hit you three times before engaging in battle.

The bully laughed and said, "One," as he punched me in the stomach. The second landed on my jaw.

Then I said, "Hurry, one more." Just as the third hit my chest, I unleashed a flurry so fast that the bully hit the ground. I said, "Pick him up!" The circle stood him up, and seeing that he still lacked humility, I blitzed him with numerous knuckle sandwiches. I saw his feet bounce off the grass as he fell, I glanced at him, and I heard him moaning as he rolled on his side. I figured that he had had enough. I turned and ran to the bus and jumped in just as the doors were closing and right before it began backing up. Brad looked at me in admiration as he handed me my books.

However, the next day was not a pleasant experience. I was called into the principal's office. When I walked in, there sat the bully's parents plus my foster mother, in addition to the principal. I scanned the bully and noticed both eyes had shiners and a lower fat lip; he never made eye contact with me. The meeting went rather quickly. From what I could figure out from the hand gestures, the bully's parents wanted me expelled, but the other grown-ups wanted both sides of the story. The bully uttered something inaudible. Next, I was asked to describe my version of the fight, but I had a hard time moving my tongue to translate my thoughts into English. I sat quietly. Then with all the mental capacity I could muster, I stated, "I am sorry." I was ready to pay the price for being at fault. At that moment, the principal stood up and explained to all the parents that he had followed me all day because I was a new student and not from the neighborhood. He said he witnessed the bully pushing me in the hall and knocking my books to the floor, and in return, I held my poise. Furthermore, he told the parents that I was more or less cornered by the bully's friends, who were fencing me in. He continued saying that he observed that I let the bully hit me three times before I struck back. He turned to the bully's parents and informed them that their son has been expelled for a week. I thought to myself, *This is not like the BIA, where the whipping of the belt came first and the questions came afterward.* The principal was a good man, and later, I became aware that he was the mayor of the town. His last name was Moran.

Through the coming days and weeks, I had several brawls, most of them lasting less than a minute. And occasionally, I would get a shiner, which I considered dishonorable, and I would make it a point to give my challenger two shiners or something equivalent in injuries.

One day, after school at the house, my foster brother challenged me to a fight. He said he could beat me up with one hand tied behind his back. That didn't make any sense to me. Why would you want to fight with just one hand? He was much bigger and stronger than me. He probably outweighed me by fifty pounds. But I was nimble and swifter. Yet I did not want to scrap with my foster brother. I had no ill will toward him. However, he continued to say things that slowly activated my inner core, which I tapped into to wage war. He brought over a roll of duct tape, and I started taping his right arm, which was his dominant side, to show me his superior status. In the meantime, my foster sister Joan was pounding on the bedroom door, demanding that Craig open the door. He pushed the bed against the door so she would not open it. Then he began seriously provoking me to fight. I began to size him up. Where could I strike him without hurting him and still make it appear serious? I launched a quick jab with my left hand that landed on the right side of his chin and slid up to his nose. This got his attention. He turned red with anger and began chasing me around the room. I knew if he got a hold of me, he would inflict some pain, so I used my agility and danced around his one-arm claw. He was yelling for me to loosen his right hand when suddenly the door came flying open as if a lightning bolt had struck it. We both went flying off in different directions. When we regained our balance, I noticed my foster father standing in the doorway. The door had completely blown off the hinges and split in two. The bed that was blocking the entry had slid completely across the bedroom.

He said with dismay in his voice, "What the hell is going on, boy?" I looked at Craig as he was trying to take the duct tape off. My foster sister Joan was crying, and my foster mother was also standing by the entry in disbelief. My foster father began taking off his belt as he was scolding Craig. I don't recall the words that were said, but it wasn't nice. He told Craig to bend over, and then he gave him one whack with his belt.

He started walking out when I said, "I need a spanking too."

He said, "Bend over," so I did, and I got hit with his belt. It was a gentle thrash compared to the boarding school smackdowns. I smiled and felt recognized as part of the family. Craig and I never got in any more fights. In fact, we hardly even spoke any unkind words toward one another the rest of our days in school and to this present day. My foster mother would tell people that I'm the only kid that asked for a "lickin'" and then smiled after getting one.

Throughout my elementary education and into high school, I was involved in numerous fights. I tried to avoid them, but sometimes the teasing was too upsetting, and I would tap into the destructive side and blow a fuse. My foster father finally said to me, "Son, there are a billion people on the earth, and there's only one of you. You can't just beat up everyone that you quarrel with. You must learn to get along with those you dislike." From that time until the present, I try to see the good in my fellow travelers on this earth's amphitheater, even if I have to turn over a stone or a leaf to find the shiny side. I have become aware of the fact that it's easier to attack and harder to understand. We are all the same even though we might be different in color on the outside, but we all bleed red on the inside. We might be from different countries, with different cultures, yet we all become one when we become the dust of Mother Earth. We are here for just a moment in time. Let's not squander it in hostility by exchanging blows. Instead, let's find joy and happiness by serving one another.

During my eighth-grade year, a neighborhood kid was selling his guitar, amplifier, and microphone for a reasonable price. I purchased them even though I never had any music lessons. The seller agreed to teach me, but he had made prior commitments that required him to leave the town. Before he left, he mentioned to some classmates that I had purchased his instruments. Subsequently I received a phone call inviting me to play with a band at the junior high assembly the following week. I stated to the caller that I had just acquired the guitar a couple of days ago and had not learned any notes. He identified himself as the bandleader. He stated that he really needed a body just to round out the band, and he promised to teach me enough chords to get me through the song that they were going to perform. I agreed to join the band as a rhythm guitarist.

On the day of the assembly, we set our equipment on the stage before the students entered the auditorium. The faculty aid that was in charge of the assembly was the junior high music teacher, Mr. Evans. He declared that before he would let us perform our number, he wanted to hear the song so he could determine if it was appropriate for the students. In the meantime, I took a ten-minute crash course learning the notes G, F, C, and D. The bandleader would nod to signal to me when to change the chords. We began playing our country rock tune when Mr. Evans interrupted us and yelled at us to stop. He said, "One of you is out of tune." He asked if we could all hit the C note, and we did, but he couldn't focus on the transgressor. He asked if we could individually strum the C note. Each band member hit the C note as requested. When it was my turn, I plucked the note proudly, then he pronounced "It's you."

By now, the seats were about to get packed. Mr. Evans uttered that he didn't have time to tune up my guitar. He suggested that instead of me leaving the stage, he would just unplug my guitar and amplifier. He articulated that I could still play with the band, but I just would not be producing any noise from my instrument. I glanced at the bandleader, and he said he was good with it. I shrugged my shoulder to give a half-hearted consent. The curtains were drawn closed when the assembly program commenced. We waited quietly for a spell. We could hear the person at the mic begin introducing the band as the curtains were drawn back, exposing us. We received a polite warm applause from the audience. The band was a little stiff and nervous as the drummer began clicking his sticks onto his drum. This jangle seemed to melt the ice off the cold fingers and loosen the leg muscles of the band members. The music was loud as it seemed to overwhelm the vocals, yet it was better than any lecture by a teacher from the podium. I began strumming my guitar and tried to blend in with the melodies by tapping my shoes.

Then I received an epiphany: The audience does not know that I am unplugged! As a band, we are here to entertain. I put that thought into action and began scooting across the floor as I raised my guitar vertically. I ran my fingers up and down the neck as I strummed excitedly on the bars! That brought a roar of approval from the spectators. I scanned quickly over to my bandleader, and he had a slight grin of support. Then I did a "Chuck Berry" imitation, with a facial expression of pain and tasting lemon for the first time that really brought the crowd out of their seats. I spotted Mr. Evans against the wall laughing as his belly was jiggling uncontrollably. No sooner than we started playing, we finished the gig. The band members joined the audience, clapping to the performance. They asked me if I could join them in the band, but I knew I was not ready for the stage, so I declined the offer.

Years later, while rehearsing for our high school graduation, a pretty little blonde girl came up to me and asked if I still play guitar. I replied, "Just now and then."

She retorted, "I remember you were really good in junior high."

I smiled and graciously said thank you. My mind drifted off as I thought of how my actions created an illusion. What this person's brain interpreted as real, based on the information received through life's experiences, was erroneous because it lacked all the facts (my guitar was unplugged). Hence, our receptions sometimes have limitations. Therefore, seek clarity and truth in all possibilities. This will lead to understanding reality—the key to transforming life.

WOLTA'II
Chapter 5

Adapting to a Different Culture

About three weeks had gone by since I began living with the Clowards, my foster family, and I was trying my best to adjust to the new way of life. One of the adaptations was the diet. I was so used to eating plenty of meat at every meal. With my new family, we ate more vegetables and sparingly animal protein, especially mutton, which I would crave often. One evening for supper, my foster mother prepared a meal that included some kind of green vegetable that tasted unbearable to me. I tried eating it, but couldn't choke it down. Everyone at the table was excused upon completing their meal. I just sat there, stirring the green slime. My foster mother insisted that I eat it, and I could not leave the table until I had consumed all that was on my plate. So I just sat there, looking at this sustenance. I am sure it was good for me, but it was so strange in texture and taste. My foster father tried to encourage me by saying, "Just close your eyes and inhale it." So I tried that approach. I took the whole helping and stuffed it in my mouth so I could hardly close it. I began gagging, and I spit it into my hand. I held it, wondering what I should do with it, and then, without wavering, I flung it into the living room, which was adjacent to the dining table. Just as the edibles left my hand, my foster mother came around the corner and saw it airborne into her living room!

She yelled at me and said, "Get in there and clean it up!"

I innocently turned to her, opened my hands, and said, "What?"

She said, "You know what! Go pick it up!"

Again, I gestured guiltlessly and said, "What?"

By now my foster father had heard the commotion and had entered the kitchen and asked, "What's the matter?" My foster mother explained the situation. He then asked, "Where is this morsel?" We all entered the living room, looking around for a green spinach-looking splatter, but to my amazement, there was no evidence of anything on the floor, ceiling, sofas, or piano—nothing. We all scanned the living room for thirty minutes when my foster mother ordered me to go straight to bed. The next morning, she was still upset with me.

She said, "You're going without breakfast today." So I left the house without eating. I figured it wasn't the first time I skipped a meal. In the back of my mind, I kept wondering where that food item could have gone. It just vanished into thin air.

After school, I walked home from the bus stop and was taken aback by the scene of all the front-room furniture out on the lawn and a couple of men dressed in white coveralls cleaning the sofas. I peeked into the living room, and it was empty—not even the curtains were hanging, nor were there any pictures on the walls. My foster father walked up behind me and said, "The woman has gone mad." No food item was ever found. But as for me and my foster mother, I knew that she knew what happened. Still, I wonder how such a matter could just dematerialize. I believe someone was watching out for me and helping me. Sometimes we do things that are not done with criminal intentions, yet we get caught between two burdensome circumstances. The best way out is to own your actions and apologize to anyone you may have offended. Over the years, I came to love my foster mother's home cooking, especially her desserts. She was well-known in that region for decorating wedding cakes. I now crave her raisin-filled cookies.

When I was approximately around the age of fourteen, one of my foster mother's relatives passed away. She asked to go see her friend at the funeral home for the viewing. I declined, but she persisted until I agreed to go. I was a little nervous because in Navajo customs, it is taboo to see a dead person. I believed this came about during the time of the smallpox plague when relatives of the deceased would get infected by coming around to pay their respects. As a result, the ominous idea of the dead became part of the tribal perception. Even so, I complied with my foster mother's wish. Afterward I began to ponder about the passage from mortality into the spiritual realm. I questioned how grueling it must be to stop breathing. Along these lines, I began holding my breath to see if I could describe the sensation. But I could never capture the feeling of transition.

However, I gained a greater awareness through the following experience. My foster mother was well-known for her baking and decorating wedding cakes. On one occasion, I walked into the kitchen, and she was right in the middle of baking and icing a cake when she asked me if I could make her some roses. With my artistic talent, I took the frosting tool and whipped out different-size roses on wax paper. When she wasn't looking, I squeezed frosting into my mouth, and I began to choke. I tried to get my foster mother's attention, but to no avail, the tables were too big around for me to tap her, and I couldn't make a sound. Then I heard a voice saying, "Get a drink of water." I walked over by the sink and started filling a glass of water when I popped out of my body! I was suspended above the ceiling. I saw a clear layer that I knew was the Sheetrock, but I was able to see right through it. I was observing everything including my body standing erect in front of the sink. The water was still running out of the faucet. I glanced at the kitchen clock that was located near the ceiling. I could see the second hand moving as usual. I looked over at my foster mother, and she was busy working on the cake. Everything was normal. I didn't have to labor for oxygen. In fact, I didn't need oxygen. Then a thought came into my mind. I wanted to go see my natural mother. I knew that I was no longer bound by the physical field. I didn't have to get into a bus and sit for ten hours to see her. All I had to do was conceive in my mind, and it would happen. A second before I was ready to project myself, I felt two beings on each side of me. They restrained me with an energy force that felt like a G-force equal to that of an aircraft ready for departure on a runway. I could hear the sound of intense energy force as I was being transported toward my body. Instantly I had returned to my body with a quake. I looked around, and everything was the same as when I was out of my body, yet this time, I was in my physical body.

I walked over to my foster mother and started to describe what had just happened to me. With excitement, I told her that I was out of my body and I was watching her from above the ceiling, but she just asked if I was finished with the roses. I again repeated with enthusiasm what had taken place, but again, she repeated word for word the same question as before, "Are you finished with the roses?" I was a little confused why she couldn't hear what I was saying. Then I realized that her eyes had a film over them, a light clear layer over her eyes. I understood that she was not supposed to know.

I stood up and said, "Your roses are done, and I came out of my body, but you're not supposed to know about that." As I walked away, I could hear her say "Thank you."

What I learned from this phenomenon is that we do not die and we are eternal beings having a human experience, spiritual souls without limitation, and physical bodies with imperfections. There is no agony when we make the transition of leaving our human existences because we are just occupying a temporary form, a shell. In fact, for some of us, it is a relief to leave our physical compositions. Through this blending of a carnal body and spiritual selves, we acquired the knowledge of what the mortal body senses from our birth to the completion of our passage. If not for this experience, we could not even know a simple matter such as what salt tastes like or the feeling of the sunrays hitting our skin. I came to understand that in the spiritual state, we are attached to our loved ones. Why else would I want to see my natural mother? I was missing her because of being away to school, and I just wanted to see her briefly. I knew that it wasn't mandatory that I ride a bus for ten hours. I could be there in an instance. At the same time, the universe is in total order. I wasn't allowed to just leave my body and go off into the wild blue yonder. I was escorted right back where I came from. Still, I wonder about what I considered solid was not so; otherwise I could not have been able to see right through the sheetrock. Thus what is real? To whom is it tangible? And for what purpose does it exist? The reality that we are spiritual beings having a human experience provides us the ability to answer these questions through our daily involvement with the world. We have the opportunity to grow from within, then share ourselves with others as we grow outwardly.

Chapter 6

Back to Roots

In the summertime, I would return home to the reservation like many who were on the Indian Placement Program as it was termed by the Church of Jesus Christ of Latter-day Saints. In Navajo, it was simply called "Gah-Mully," I don't know what that means, but everyone understood it as the "Mormons." As I grew older, I began to realize that in both cultures, the White man's and Natives', beliefs were diverse. For example, my natural mother prized turquoise jewelry over diamonds, and my foster mother the opposite. My foster father's daily task corresponded with his wristwatch, and my natural father went about his duties according to the sun and the moon. If I were to switch the values with my parents, they would be perplexed but not totally hopeless. Likewise, I would switch my thoughts and actions to my location. I would describe my dilemma by using a sports analogy. When I was with my foster family, I played by football rules, and when I returned to be with my natural family, I would play by basketball rules. I could not use football rules to play basketball or vice versa. This manner of thinking kept me from being confused or discouraged. I would take a few moments to make the transition in my mind, from living with modern amenities with all the comforts of life to the challenges of existing on the reservation. I would compare it to a deep sea diver, having to decompress before resurfacing to normal atmospheric pressure.

Yet, I still had hurdles that I had to overcome. One of those instances was my language. After spending ten months of not speaking Navajo, I would forget how to express myself to my father. Everyone else in my family knew how to speak English except for my father. He said to me once, "God made me a Navajo and gave me a tongue to speak Navajo, so that's who I am. If you want to talk to me, speak Navajo." Navajo is one of the hardest languages to be fluent in. I was able to process what was being said in Navajo, but I couldn't get my tongue to articulate my thoughts. At first, when I was young, I just wouldn't say anything, but as I grew older, I knew I had to relearn as quickly as possible due to the short summer period at home, so I would take my little brother Lewis behind the house and we would practice speaking a whole conversation until I memorized the discussion. Then I would go and have a dialogue with my father. Sometimes he would chuckle, but he understood I was trying. As for my older siblings, they would tease me and call me the little White boy because my accent was that of a White man.

I have a brother named Howard who is eight years older than me and who is mentally challenged. My mother told me that when he was born, the nurses dropped him on his head, and he was slower in learning things because of it, and he had a hard time hearing. Consequently, we developed a unique sign language that is not recognizable by anyone. We would talk all day and night without uttering a sound and that lingo I never forgot. Howard always kept me grounded and reminded me of my roots just by his authentic untainted nature. In the summer, we would ride horses all day, pretending that we were working cattle or herding sheep, but we were just enjoying life one day at a time. On one occasion while riding near a wash, he sighted an eagle feather on the edge of a cliff. I offered to descend down the sandy ridge and get the feather. As I eased my way along the rim, I notice the ground was unstable with loose sand. Without notice, the earth began moving like an avalanche. I quickly grabbed onto a clump of sandstone near me. I could feel the dirt slowly eroding from underneath me, and soon the sandstone that I was using as my anchor started sliding as well. I motioned to my brother to throw a rope to me. Meanwhile, I grabbed onto a cluster of grass. I could see the rope flying over my head, and I just couldn't time it to where I could let go of my security of the grass and seize the rope. Then the whole ground began rumbling down off the cliff. As I was sliding, I gave one last ditch effort to grasp another batch of grass. I laid there at the border of the overhang with my feet dangling over the edge. I dared not move while trying to think of what I could do next. I had slid too far down to use the rope as a lifeline, yet my brother kept tossing it repeatedly. I laid there for what seemed like eternity as time slowed, and I could feel the updraft of the breeze. Then without warning, like a trap door, everything just unleashed, and I fell with it. It was so sudden that I didn't have the responsiveness to react. The next thing I knew was my brother throwing water in my face. I regained consciousness and started moving my toes and arms to see if I was all in one piece. I was lucky that I fell onto mountains of sand that had accumulated from the wind at the bottom of the wash. I sat up and tried getting my composure when my brother asked, "Where's the eagle feather?" I gazed up at the cliff and realized that I was fortunate to endure the fall without any broken bones, just scratches and a mouth full of sand and dirt. As for the eagle feather, it was lost in all the debris. My thoughts drifted into the clouds as I sat covered in sand. I thought of how we sometimes we get caught up looking at some shiny object in a showcase—a car, jewelry, clothes etc.—then without much planning, we convince ourselves that we have to have it. Our actions in obtaining the prize are usually feeble. Without pure enthusiastic energy, we get exhausted and give up feeling disappointed. Yet, our lives were worth living and fulfilled prior to seeing the shimmering object.

Chapter 7

My Spiritual side experience

I often wonder why we sometimes put ourselves in jeopardy for our love ones. Is it an act of bravery or foolishness? Or is it neither? In the incident of the "eagle feather fall," I didn't want my brother to take the risk of falling due to his health issues. I figured I was more agile and limber to retrieve the eagle feather. Besides, I would rather be in pain than watch him in agony. I would call it an act of brotherly love. Other times when we proceed in vain, we end up overwhelmed as in this next incident I experienced at sixteen when I was a sophomore in high school.

Spanish Fork High School in 1969 consisted of three grades: sophomores, juniors, and seniors. So as sophomores, we were at the bottom of the totem pole as far as respect and privileges from upper classmates went. Opportunities to join clubs were scarce. As a result, when I was asked to join a club that wasn't identified as an acclaimed club of the school, I was interested but tentative. The majority of the members consisted of malcontents. Nevertheless, I went along with some of their initiations, which was more embarrassing than noble. I told my foster brother who was a senior about this club, and he responded by saying that it was not a good group and I should avoid being seen with them. I ignored his advice, which I would regret later. As part of their fundraisers, the club had a beer party and charged the students a fee for each cup of beer they consumed. I was asked to be a bartender along with several other aspirants. The bash took place in a remote canyon on a Saturday night. There were several hundred students who surrounded a big bonfire that could be seen from a long distance. The glow from the fire reflected onto the sides of the canyon. My job was to sell each cup of beer for fifty cents. Of course, no ID was required. As the evening grew darker, the bonfire grew brighter. Then I heard a commotion, and several students were laughing as they pointed into the inferno. For some reason, I left my post and began walking toward the fire to see what the uproar was all about. When I glanced into the fire, I noticed a black object succumbing to the heat, and without caution, I reached into the fire and grabbed this article, which turned out to be a Bible and Book of Mormon combination handbook. My arms and hands were not burned, not even singed though the fire was emitting blistering heat. The students were stunned, watching as I brushed the charcoal off the pamphlet. I put the booklet into my shirt pocket; then I spoke words that I would not think to say if I was trying to be accepted by this club. I chastised whoever threw the Bible into the fire and proclaim this book as a history of my people. Then I walked back to the bar area as a quiet stillness gripped the onlookers. I told my friend, "This is not a good place. Let's go." He agreed, but we had no ride.

As fortune would have it, a tall lanky student overheard our conversation and said, "I'm leaving now, and I can give you a ride home." He had the coolest car in school, as I recall. It was a 1957 Chevrolet Bel Air with a 327 engine. It was every teenager's dream car. He made some donuts as we spun around in circles in a cloud of smoke from the tires. Then he pushed down on the horn, and the sound of a roadrunner blasted from the hood. We left the scene, fishtailing down the narrow winding highway flying at breakneck speed.

I sat in the front middle seat mystified by all the action. Then we hit the side of the hill and almost went over the edge. The tires were screeching as the driver overcorrected and hit the bank again. This time, we ricocheted straight off the road into the dark abyss. I recollect the silence as I observed the moon and stars in the sky and the tops of the pine trees below us as we quietly sailed over them. I thought to myself, *This must be what it must feel like to be in a flying saucer.* That was the last thing I remember.

I woke up in a strange dark, cold, wet space without oxygen. I fumbled around trying to get my sense of balance. I swiped at the darkness and realized it was water that had filled the cab. I saw shades of lights reflecting off the water as my eyes starting getting used to the blackness. I noticed a body floating by me, and I realized that we had crashed off the cliff and landed in a river. I tried pulling on the door handle, but the door was too mangled. I was overcome with deep thoughts about my life, and I reckoned that I was about to drown. I thought about my natural parents and how sad they would be when they received the news. I thought of my foster parents and how I would disappoint them. I thought of leaving this life at such a young age. I was supposed to get married and have children and grandchildren. I was supposed to go to college. I told myself, "What a waste of life." As I reflected on my life, a surge of energy consumed my being, and I said to myself, "I am not dying!" I heard a voice telling me to open the wing. I felt along the side of the door until I reached the wing. Then I was told to pull the wing apart. I thought, *I can hardly get my head in the wing. What about my shoulders and the rest of my body?*

I heard the voice again with more firmness saying, "Pull it!" I grabbed with both hands inside the frames of the wings without doubt and all the energy I could muster. I spread apart the steel frame. I was instructed again by the voice to put my head into the opening. I did not question the voice anymore. I stuffed my head into the opening. Then something happened to my body that I cannot explain. My body transformed into a shape that felt like an eel. I slithered through the wing and began swimming toward the top of the current. I knew something was very unusual with my body; I could not see my arms. I tried looking at my form, but I was not allowed to. I swam by moving from side to side until I reached the top of the water. When I inhaled the air, my figure returned to the human physique instantly. I grabbed onto the frame of the car next to the passenger side near the tires. I heard someone say, "How many more are in there?"

I said, "Three!" Just then, the car ignited, but it was swiftly extinguished by the river. A number of boys jumped onto the car with rocks and began smashing the windows. I turned and glanced into the river and noticed three rainbow trout observing all the commotion. I let go of the car and swam to shore.

As I sat on a rock trying to make sense of all that had just taken place, my friend swam next to me. We sat next to each other without saying a word. Then I said, "I don't think this club is worth it."

Then my friend said, "We're on the wrong side of the river. We need to swim back across." So we jumped back into the river, and for the first time, I felt the crispy cold water that had melted from the spring runoffs. The flow of the river was strong and swift, but we managed to make our way back to the other side of the river where the cars were parked. I noticed a somber crowd as some thought we didn't make it. They all stared at the wreckage not knowing that we were part of the accident. Nevertheless, we were without a ride again. Then as before another classmate said, he would give us a ride home, and off we went without any fanfare. I walked into the house all soaked and let my foster mother know that I was home. She acknowledged my return and said good night.

I hesitated for a minute. Then I worked up some courage and tried to rationalize the incident in my mind before uttering a few simple words, "I got in a wreck."

She looked a little bewildered and said, "Good night." I was taken aback by her lack of alarm. I knelt by her side and noticed that she had a glaze over her eyes, and then I understood that she was not to be aware of the accident. I stood up and started walking away, describing the crash as I went. I turned around waiting for reaction with no luck.

At that moment, I whispered, "Good night."

And to my disbelief, she heard me and responded, "Good night." I walked upstairs to my bedroom and started taking off my damp clothes when I noticed something in my pocket. I managed to work it out of my pocket, and it was the Bible that I had pulled from the fire. It was charred on the edges, but I could still read the inner pages.

I thought to myself, *Thank goodness I saved you from the fire, as I believe you saved my life.*

There were many sleepless nights that I spent following the accident. Sometimes I would wonder if it really occurred, but all I have to do is look at my right thumb where a two-inch scar is visible from pushing the wing apart. I wear the mark to this day. I use it as a reminder just how fragile life is and to always be grateful for every breath. It is the most valuable element we have.

WOLTA'II

Chapter 8

Moving Forward to Adulthood

Having had various experiences that encompass the paranormal and spiritual field throughout my youth, one would think I was indestructible and without limitations. But because I am half human, I continued to make blunders in my judgments as this next story demonstrates.

During the spring of my sophomore year, the Indian Placement Program gave a party for all the students at an amusement park named Lagoon. It is located north of Salt Lake City, Utah. My caseworker, Harold Reynolds, was an admirable man. He encouraged me to attend the event; he said that it would be good for me to hang out with some native kids. As a result, I agreed and hopped in with three other students that lived in towns near my area. We didn't know each other, but we all dressed the same—wrangler pants, long-sleeved western shirts, and cowboy boots. We arrived at Lagoon uneventfully and began wandering around the park when the oldest minor had an idea. He said that we needed to meet some girls. His plan was that we all put five dollars into a pot and whoever brought a girl back to the exact spot first would win twenty dollars. I was a shy kid around girls, except the ones I call my friends at school who I had known for years. Reluctantly I agreed and deposited my five dollars. I had no idea how I was going get a girl to that location first, but I wanted the twenty dollars. When the kid said, "Go!" I took off racing in the opposite direction from the three. I ran down the sidewalk and jumped over some hedges, and I saw a girl sitting on a bench by herself. I startled her, when I skidded to a stop next to her and began stuttering out words about twenty dollars and I would split it with her if she would just go with me. Then I beheld her face and eyes. The whole world stopped spinning, and time stood still. I saw the most beautiful girl in the universe. As a young man that had never dated, I knew this was the girl I was going to marry. The least of my worries now was the twenty dollars. When she spoke, it sounded like a mouth harp. She said she couldn't go because she was babysitting.

I asked, "Where's the baby?" She pointed at a small baby carrier next to her. I sat down and asked her name.

She said, "Marge" (not her real name to protect the innocent). I asked her other mindless questions. I have no idea how long I was there when her sister walked up and introduced herself. I jumped up, and in my nervous state, something came out of my mouth, but it was no harp. She had a kind gentle smile.

She said, "I'll pay for your rides and some treats." She then handed her sister twenty dollars! The rest of the day went by rapidly yet magical as I seemed to be the observer of my own activities. It appeared as if I was inside a sphere. I could hear echoes of laughter and chatter from the roller coasters and other rides. The day ended, but not before I promised her that I would see her again.

Over the years, we would see one another on different occasions. These were unplanned, but we ended up at the same events. Some were at BYU dances that we were too young to attend but somehow managed to get in. I talked her into going with me to the prom during my senior year. I had her high on a pedestal and treated her as if she was made of the most exquisite treasures. Yet I was sideswiped by an aggressive girl who came out of nowhere. I was taken aback by her charge. Due to my laid-back nature, I didn't know how to reject this girl, and I was confused and troubled. I believe there must be opposition in all things, but sometimes we get too close to the forest and cannot see the trees. Fortunately, I had the Holy Spirit, the universal energy, however way you want to illustrate it. I was blessed with it. This energy helped me clarify my confusion through a vivid dream one night. Everything was distinct; the message was apparent. I dreamed I was standing at the edge of a beige marble surface, next to a slow-moving green river. I sensed that it was very powerful. There was steam rising from the water. I observed a naked girl swimming in the river. It was the aggressive girl. She was splashing and urging me to jump in, saying the water feels good. Then I looked across the river and saw many pretty girls standing in a line. Some would smile, others would wave, and some were brushing their hair, while others were manicuring their fingernails. I looked up the line and noticed they were all standing in the direction of a large throne that was made of gold. There was a beautiful girl sitting on the throne wearing an elegant white robe that draped around the chair and rested on the ground. She had long black hair. She sat stoic with both arms resting at her side. I tried getting her attention, but I was made aware that this was a significant state of affairs and there was no room for philandering. I recognized the young woman sitting on the throne as Marge. I understood by her expression that if I was to be with her, I needed to elevate my substance. That was the end of my dream.

I translated the dream as a powerful message about my future with a mate. I had been shown two ways of life to choose. One didn't require much self-discipline, while the other demanded self-mastery. One woman frolicked in ways of the world, as represented by her nakedness in the water, while the other reigned with modest intense strength, as symbolized by her sitting on a gold throne dressed in a pure white robe. Having experienced a challenging life up to the age of eighteen, I had now put myself in a position where I was using my free agency to create a world without much planning. There was an abundance of opportunities, and time was standing still. Unwisely, I was taking everything for granted. I squandered a full-ride scholarship to Brigham Young University. I attended only a half-semester and transferred to Utah Technical College. My dream proved to be factual as I fell into the green slow powerful river with the naked girl. Life became an uphill battle. I never made it across the river. I lacked the capacity necessary to make it to the gold throne. My inferior choices fragmented all aspiration for life experience with Marge.

Even though we make miscalculations in our lives, the Holy Spirit never leaves us. No matter how unworthy we might feel about his presence, even when we deny his existence, he is constantly attending to our well-being, as illustrated in this next narrative.

I had been married over a year and had a little girl. I was attending college. We returned to the reservation for a weekend visit with my in-laws. We left late to return back to school. It was around two o'clock in the morning as we passed through Monticello, Utah. It had just snowed that day and there was three feet of snow pushed on the edges of the road. It was a clear night without any clouds and with a full moon. You could see the sparkles on the snow from the light of the moon. The snow had melted off the roads. Not wanting to be late for class, I was speeding in a brand-new Grand Torino when all of a sudden, the car shut off. I let it coast to a stop, I turned the key, and it started back up. I began driving, and when I got up to fifty miles per hour, it shut off again. I let the car rest for a few minutes. I turned the key, and the car started up again. I had driven a short distance and not over twenty miles per hour when the car shut off for the third time. By now, my wife woke up and questioned, "Is everything okay?"

I said, "Yes," but not in a convincing voice. I let the car sit again for a few minutes. I turned the key, and the car fired up without issues. At this point, I felt fortunate that we were just moving five miles per hour when I noticed two enormous men standing on the side of the road. They were dressed in bulky leather and fur clothing, their boots were laced up to their knees, their coats had hoods like the Eskimos, their coats draped down to their thighs, and they had large gloves that had fur to their elbows. They had massive shoulders, and their height was easily over seven feet, maybe eight feet tall. Their eyes were piercing black, their smiles were peaceful, and they cast off a feeling of benevolence. I asked my wife, as we were coasting by the giants, "Do you see what I'm seeing?"

She said, "Yes."

I asked again, "What do you see?"

She said, "Two large men." I had to lower my head to the dashboard to see their full head. As we slid by them, I noticed there was black ice on the road!

I thought, There's no way we could've made the turn if we were traveling at the original rate of speed, even at fifty miles per hour. Then it dawned on me that the two men were messengers from ancient times. I quickly stopped the car. We hadn't gone over twenty yards. I got out of the car and ran to the exact location where the men were standing. But there were no signs of them anywhere! I spent the next forty-five minutes walking back and forth, yelling and looking for footprints in vain. I was trying to open a channel of communications by screaming, "Come on back. I have a lot of questions." Even if they were to return, I doubt one could've fit into the car.

The more I contemplate the two men, the more I realize I do not have the capability to comprehend the reasons how beings can be there one minute and disappear the next, in addition why they show themselves in the first place. Still, I felt honored to have seen them, especially after making so many missteps. I thought I was banished from any spiritual experiences. Henceforth, I felted exonerated and fortunate to be back in the inspiring marvelous circle.

Chapter 9

Preparing for Life, Career

College education had its challenges, mostly from the financial sector. Since forfeiting a scholarship to BYU, I had a difficult time finding any funding for my education. Nevertheless, I proceeded forward doing whatever it took to get a seat in the classroom. On occasions, I received help from my student friends that were on scholarships that bought their school supplies. They would hint that they needed a new pair of welding gloves even though theirs appeared practically new. I would dig them out of the trash bin after they discarded them. Fortunately, I had an artistic talent painting. I sold my artwork at a local thrift store, and in addition, I worked welding gas tanks full-time at nights. There were many nights that I went to bed hungry. My driving force was the fact that I did not want to return to the reservation to herd sheep. After a year in the trade school, I received my first break in the welding field. I was offered a chance to attend a ground-breaking school, of all places, on the Navajo Reservation.

A joint alliance with the AFL-CIO, Pipefitters and Plumbers UA Local Union 469 Phoenix, Arizona, and UA

Local Union 412 Albuquerque, New Mexico, along with the Navajo Nation and Bechtel Corporation, formed a welding school in Window Rock, the capital of the Navajo Nation. During this period, there were several coal-fired power plants being erected on and nearby the Navajo Reservation. The bulk of the coal for the power plants was also being mined from the Reservation, and as a result, the Navajo tribe stipulated that skilled Navajo labor be used to man the construction jobs on the power plants. For this reason, my opportunity to get into the union became obtainable.

The Navajo Nation furnished a vacant building that was on the fairgrounds. It was actually an old barn. The Bechtel Corporation supplied the pipes for welding and welding machines. UA Local 469 provided the teacher for the classroom, and UA Local 412 offered the welding instructor. It was a demanding crash course.

Every entity involved insisted on immediate results and wanted to claim the credit for the feat. It was the first time since boarding school that I was alongside of my Navajo brothers. Although we were being pushed daily, we still had time for recreation. The boys made a homemade basketball hoop and backboard. At lunchtime, we would play suicide basketball. We would choose a partner, and the first team to twenty wins. There was little dribbling, and we played it like rugby. If your teammate rebounded the ball, you were fair game to get tackled. No one cried foul. We were like an Eveready Battery; you would take a hit and keep on ticking, no whining or flopping like the pros.

In five months, five of us were picked to take the UA Welding test in Phoenix, Arizona. The test consisted of two welding procedures: a two-inch and a ten-inch schedule 80 carbon steel pipe with a backing ring, welded with 7018 electrodes. Four straps would be cut and bent. If there were any flaws in the welds, the straps would break. The weld would not pass. We were given notice prior to taking the test that if we failed, we were not allowed to return to the school and that we would be out on the street. On the other hand, if we passed the test, we would be taken in as an apprentice and begin a five-year apprenticeship program with UA Local 469 Phoenix. In addition, we would be placed as a pipefitter welder on one of the power plants that was being constructed near or on the Navajo Reservation at that time.

Having been selected to take the welding test, I was thrilled. I knew I only had one chance. I practiced unrelentingly, yet I was familiar with another unseen influence that was crucial to attaining success, through prayer. I contemplated who could I asked for a blessing. I wanted a spiritual man, not a religious man—an authentic man without loyalty to any denomination. I turned to my father. I believe that all fathers have the privilege to bless their children with authority from God, who is our Father in heaven. Thus, I drove to my folks' house. It was evening by the time I arrived at the rock house out in the middle of an oasis, away from the worldly noise and confusion. I was welcomed with smiles, hugs, and a warm cup of tea.

My mother was a person that came right to the point and asked, "Why are you here so late?"

I said, "I came here to ask for a blessing."

Without hesitation, she turned to my father and said, "You have been called upon to make holy, this plea."

My father lowered his head and reverently asked, "Why do you summons me for a blessing?"

I explained, "I have been selected to take a welding test that would have a great influence on my life. Also, I have worked hard for this one opportunity."

My father sat quietly meditating for a time that seem awkwardly long. Then he rose up to his feet and said, "I will take you to a place where you can pray for yourself." He reached into a sacred medicine bundle that was sanctified by holy men. He pulled out a buckskin pouch. Carefully he opened it and selected small turquoise and coral stones. To say it simply, turquoise is a bringer of good fortune. Coral relates to the blood of life, the beating of a heart and the rich warmth of the sun. They are truly hallowed to the Navajo people. He said, "These precious gems we'll use for offerings." Again, he reached into the medicine bundle, and this time, he brought out a pouch that contained corn pollen.

Corn pollen to Navajos is a sacred meaning of life. When performing prayers with corn pollen, the person praying takes a pinch of the pollen with his thumb and index finger and puts some at the whorl or crown of their heads, where the spirit entered the body, and places some pollen on their tongue, to speak holy words, and makes a motion toward the East, to symbolize the holy path of life.

When my father had gathered all the sacred items, he wrapped a piece of handkerchief around his head and lit a mountain tobacco. We began hiking east. I followed behind as he walked swiftly. He began chanting under his breath while smoking. He turned and gave some tobacco to me to clear my mind. We had walked about a mile when he stopped and looked to the south and then turned to the north. He said that we must keep walking. He repeated this three more times. When we were close, he put out his arms, and one pointed toward a mountain. He then took note of where his opposite arm was pointing. He said, "We're very close." He began walking as if he was stalking prey. He finally stopped and said, "This is the place." He stood as if his body was a compass. His right arm pointed south to the tip of Star Mountain, and his left arm pointed north to a tip of a mesa. He explained, "In ancient times, this was a sacred trail that was used by holy messengers. The path has a magnetic field making our prayers powerful."

The moon had an orange glow, and there was calmness in the air when he took out the turquoise and coral stones and placed them delicately under a sagebrush. "These precious stones are tokens of our gratitude for what we are about to receive," he exclaimed. We stood facing east, and with the corn pollen in our hands, we began our prayer by addressing the almighty creator of all the universes. Word for word, I repeated every phrase in Navajo that my father spoke. When I would mispronounce or skip a word, he didn't stop; he continued as if he was in a trance. The prayer was almost like lyrics in a song. It was a most humbling experience. I felt the force of the unforeseen consume my bosom. When we had concluded the supplication, we repeated these words, "It is good again" four times. This blessed phrase is to say, "Thank you," for already receiving what you just prayed for.

Following the event, the result of the prayer was unmistakable. Out of the five students that took the weld test, I was the only one that passed the two-inch and ten-inch coupons. One went on a drinking beige and never showed up at the test lab. The other three passed the ten-inch test only. Out of the three, two were held back for six months due to their lack of grasping mathematics. One transferred to UA Local 412 where they didn't require a turn-out examination at the end of the apprenticeship program. I ended up being the first to complete my apprenticeship from the welding school. Many more followed and gained a livelihood for themselves and their families.

I was fortunate and proud to work over thirty years as a Steamfitter Journeyman out of UA Local 469, Phoenix, Arizona. I worked as a welder and in managements on several nuclear power plants throughout the country, as well as many coal-fired power plants and co-gens, along with a variety of other industries like oil refineries, hospitals, semiconductor plants, schools, etc. I've made lifetime friends and acquaintances, across the USA. At the time of this writing, I am still enjoying welding at a fabrication shop in Phoenix, Arizona. Having been truly blessed with steady hands and young eyes, I give thanks for the special blessing on that special evening with my father.

Chapter 10

Sidetracks

From 1985 to 2000, I took fifteen years away from my trade and started a small business venture on the Navajo Reservation. I had put in ten years in the pipefitting industries, and I was a certified journeyman welder. But I began looking for new challenges in my life. I secured my pension credits with the union and officially retired.

One day, I was driving down Main Street in the sleepy little town of Snowflake, Arizona, USA, when I noticed a sign that read, "Video Rentals." I made a U-turn and pulled next to a small one-room building. I knocked on the door, and a bright smiley faced man greeted me with a hardy handshake. I asked him if he could enlighten me about his business with the video rentals. For the next few minutes, he articulated how things operated. My mind was already spinning; I envisioned what this would mean for my people on the reservation. This was my chance to return to the reservation and help them. I thought of how a family could come together in front of a television for two hours and not experience violence, or forget the poverty, the unemployment, and drug addictions. I asked the gentleman how I could get into this business.

He replied, "I can help you get started." Right there and then, we began a business over a handshake. We didn't know one another, but I knew this was a good man, an intelligent and honorable trusting man.

I was naive. I had no experience or education in running a business. Nonetheless, I believed in myself. I knew that if I could see it with my mind's eye, then I could make it come to pass. Plus, I had positive energy and stamina. Still, I didn't realize the multifaceted structures of a bureaucratic system in dealing with the tribal and federal government on the reservation. I asked, "How complicated can it be to start a video rental business?" I was in for the ride of my life. Time didn't exist in that setting. There were no deadlines. Money was a secondary issue. This society was existing on requiring all who enter their domain to bring all documents to their offices for inspection according to their by-laws. It didn't matter how trivial or absurd the issues were. In addition, both the federal and tribal offices required they get the original copies of any documents. There is much to write about that took place during that fifteen years, but I will condense it to one chapter since the trials are basically the same with any business ventures on the reservations.

Chapter 11

Entrepreneur on the Reservation

Lesson one, the reservation is federal land. If you want to live there you must lease a plot. If you want to do business on the Rez, you need a business site lease. If you want to do anything on the Rez, you need a lease agreement with the federal government. Where the Bureau of Indian Affairs (BIA) leaves off, the Navajo tribal government takes over as far as bureaucratic approaches. My first business location on the reservation was an eye opener to these requirements.

I completed a survey of the location in Fort Defiance, Arizona, USA, that looked desirable for a business and found an elderly gentleman that had the base lease. We agreed to the terms for rent and made arrangements to have a mobile home set up as the business structure. Why a mobile home? If you build a permanent building on federal land, you will more than likely lose it when your lease expires. I brought in a single wide trailer and secured it down with railroad ties. I had set a date for a grand opening, and I could tell the residents were eager and were as excited as I was. When the final week arrived, I was visited by the regional BIA official. He refused to approve my business. He said I was too close to the road. I needed to move my trailer ten feet back from the road. Because I was out of compliance with the parameter, the man from the BIA declared that I would not be issued a permit to operate a business. I notified the individual that my grand opening was going to be Thursday of that week and to send his biggest man because all I have left was fifty dollars after spending all my savings. Consequently, my business was not recognized as a legitimate firm. Nevertheless, Thursday arrived, and I opened the doors for business.

I had no electricity because I had no permit to operate. However, the residents were lined up for a block. I ran an extension cord from the gas station that was next door to light up a single-bulb lamp that I located in the middle of the room. Customers did not care about the dim lighting. This was the Rez. We didn't have to go first class. At the end of the night, after closing, I took inventory of the equipment and movies. I had rented all my TVs and VCRs. There were only four hundred movies left; we had rented 1,600 movies! After cleaning up and sending the employees home, I had several grocery bags full of cash. I dumped them on the floor and tossed the money into the air as if it was play money. I had made more money in one night than a week's paycheck working construction. I knew from that moment that I had to diversify as quickly as possible. I opened the next video store two months later. Four months following, I opened in two locations at the same time. Up to now, I relied on the Navajo small business to assist me in complying with all the guidelines. I began running into some obstacles within the business circle when I began considering opening the fifth store in one year. The swift pace slowed down considerably due to one manager that was hesitant to cooperate.

During this pause, I hired a CPA. I was burning the candle on both ends. Some days, I would forget to eat. I was working twenty-four seven without sleep. I was operating on adrenaline rush. Acquiring a CPA was a good move. I continued to battle in the field while he paid the bills and kept the money shielded for operation of the business. I opened the fifth store with a little delay within the year.

After observing, I realized that I had a business in all the shopping centers throughout the reservation except for one. I was unable to convince the shopping center manager to let me open in the last location. He was nonresponsive to my plea. So I looked at a small plot of land located in a small town that was on my route when I did my rounds. I imagined that it would be a good pit stop to break up the wearisomeness of the drive between the stores.

I put together a business package that I knew would be satisfactory to present to the town administrators. My approach was indescribable to those who have never operated a business on a reservation. I was notified that I was on the agenda at the "Chapter House," a multiuse building on the reservation. I arrived early and made sure that I was still on the agenda. I sat down next to a white-haired old gentleman who spoke very good English. We introduced ourselves according to our clans, and I found out that he was my father within the clan structure. Then we shook hands again but with more value in our grips. The meeting began with a word of prayer, which is practiced in all events on the reservation. I looked around the room and counted thirteen individuals sitting in attendance. Mostly elderly folks were there to share a meal afterward, also a custom following get-togethers. I began reflecting on how much time and money I had at stake riding on these thirteen people who didn't have a clue nor cared about my predicament. My name was called out, and I introduced myself as if I were addressing a mass of two hundred. When I had completed my presentation, time was set aside for inquiry about my business venture. One elderly woman was concerned that I would block her sheep and goats from forging along the road. I assured her that I am only seeking one-third of an acre and her sheep and goats would not starve. Another well-dressed woman stood up and declared that I was not from that area, that I was a stranger asking for land, and why should they agree to help me. I kept calm and tried to assure the thirteen souls that I meant no harm, when up came the old man with whom I had a brief conversation prior to the beginning of the meeting. He proclaimed, "This is my son. He is no stranger. This is his homeland. He has every right to set up a business." He continued by saying, "We send our kids to school to get an education. We tell them to come back and make things better on the reservation. I say give him the land and let him start a Navajo-owned business." I was amazed about how deep and true the old man's feelings reverberated through the audience.

A motion was made for a vote. The result was seven to six in my favor, thanks to my clan father. I was granted a business site from the Navajo tribe, but when it came up for approval with the BIA, it was contested due to the environmental assessment made by the Navajo Nation. The BIA would not recognize the tribe's qualification to perform environmental assessments. Hence, my application to operate a business for that plot of land was mothballed while the dispute was addressed in Washington, DC. After nearly a year, I was notified by the BIA that I could continue with my business. A month later, I opened for business using the same mobile trailer that I used to start my original store. I conducted business in that location for over thirteen years, one year for each individual in attendance that day it was approved by a slim majority.

During this time, I was still pursuing the last shopping center for a business lease. Time kept pressing forward, and a new opportunity materialized. With the video rental business decelerating, I turned to my partner, and we formed a rodeo filming company. We were eager to conduct this venture because of being accustomed to that lifestyle, even though neither one of us had any clue how to produce, market, and distribute the rodeo sport on videos. I must admit I did not have the time to put into this company. Thus when it was incorporated, I was designated the head camera man. After months of educating ourselves about cameras, voice overs, splicing tapes, and finding a market, we felt we were ready for our first trial run.

We decided that the Navajo Nation Fair would be an ideal starting location. The Navajo people's beloved sport is rodeo, and the fair, welcoming over 200,000 individuals daily, would be an excellent place for exposure. We ventured as a thirteen-man crew to Window Rock, Arizona,

USA, the capital of the Navajo Nation. We arrived early to give ourselves time to run cables and test the sound system. I was given notice that I needed to pay a fee to the Navajo tribe for operating any cameras on the fairground premises. I promptly got in line and noticed the fee was fifty dollars. I watched a photographer from France pay his fee. Then it was my turn. When I approached the desk where a lady was collecting the money, she looked on her sheet and said that I needed to talk with the fair manager. She was not allowed to collect any fees from me. She stated that he could be found at the rodeo grounds in a camper trailer. I managed to find his trailer and knocked on the door. A burly man opened the door. I introduced myself and explained that according to the lady who was taking the fifty-dollar fee, I needed to see him. He looked agitated, and he began verbalizing that I had been ripping off the Navajo people and my fee to film on the fairgrounds would $1,500. I answered that this filming company had not operated as business and this was our first chance to do so. I stated that this is a great free promotional tool for the Navajo Nation and its tourism sector. In addition, I questioned why a man from France was allowed to pay $50 and as a Navajo entrepreneur, my fee is $1,500. Where was the Navajo preference? The dialogue was all in vain. He took an irrational stand and wasn't moving. As a result I went to the crew and explained what had taken place. I said we could pay the fee of $1,500, but it was not right, so we're not filming. We were all disappointed and left dejected. We never returned to film on the reservation again.

One day, out of the clear blue, approximately a year after the Navajo Nation fair incident, I received a phone call from the manager of the shopping center. He made mention that he would offer the space that I have been pursuing for five years, on one condition—that we had to open in two weeks! I said that's impossible. He declared take it or leave it. I had wanted that space for a long time. I even drew a picture of exactly how the store would look five years prior. I took a deep breath and proclaimed that we would be open in two weeks. I signed the lease and turned to my executive manager for all location and stated we're opening in two weeks. I knew this was a political promotional stunt. The tribal administration had various issues with the people that I had no desire to get involved. I asked no questions and wanted no explanations. Our plan was to shut down a store that was located in southern New Mexico and relocate everything to the new store. In the meantime, we began installing carpet and shelves. We were working around the clock, and I was pushing the workers trying to meet the deadline.

We were all stressed out when I received a call from the police that my business van was involved in an accident. I rushed to the scene and noticed the van was on its side. The driver was my niece, who was my executive manager. She had been transported to the hospital. There was debris all over the road, hundreds of movies were scattered about, and drivers were pulling off the side of the road and grabbing movies by the arm full. But that was not my concern at that moment. Before I went to the hospital, I asked my staff to clean up the wreckage and salvage what they could.

My niece was lucky that she only received a couple of cuts and some bruises. She was released a few hours later.

I had a meeting with my workers and voiced that we would not work in a panic anymore. We would open when we were ready. I covered the store windows with newspapers so no one was able to see our progress. During the day of the grand opening, many tribal dignitaries were at the shopping center, and there was free food for all. I urged my workers to not attend any events and promised that I would treat them to a steak dinner when we completed the store.

The sun was beginning to set, and the festivities were winding down when we heard someone knocking on the door. I opened the door, and I noticed it was the same burly man that was the manager at the Navajo Nation fairgrounds the previous year. I said, "Can I help you?" He began muttering about running out of blank tapes and that the chairman was about to give a speech and that he desperately needed a blank tape. I stated that all the accessories were boxed up. He pleaded once again that he was in dire need of a blank tape. I responded that I would look and see if I could find one. I unpacked and opened a box that had cases of blank tapes. I returned to the front door with a blank tape in my hand. Just as he reached into his wallet for some money, I said, "It'll cost you $1,500 for the same reason you stated at the Navajo Nation Fair, that you are ripping off the Navajo people." He lowered his eyes. He understood exactly what I was insinuating from my previous transaction with him at the fairgrounds a year earlier. His hands began to tremble. I couldn't handle the suffering this man was showing. I felt uneasy and unfulfilled. I handed him the blank tape and declared, "This is on me. You don't owe me any money." I do not consider this incident an act of revenge, but rather a lesson that if you continue to repeat negative aspirations, you will eventually make a full circle and end up where you began with little progress. This lesson about treating your fellow humans as you would like to be treated echo in my heart and mind to this day.

I eventually closed my businesses down after fifteen years. I had to face my own financial challenges. I dismissed my CPA when bills were being paid late and taxes were in the rears. I made a plea deal with the IRS and agreed to a payment plan, but the Navajo tribe refused to grant me time to settle with the IRS. I was given thirty days to vacate all business properties. I would ponder often how an unbelievable amount of time and energy is spent to stay positive and focused. To wait five years to open a store and then with a stroke of a pen, it could be smothered instantly. I sold one location to a family member and gave another site to one of my daughters and her husband. The rest of the locales I liquidated to pay toward my balance with the IRS. From time to time, I will drive by where one of the stores was located. All I see is a vacant lot or empty storefronts.

There are matters better left unsaid and unwritten. What happens on the Rez stays on the Rez. Ultimately, I paid my entire debt with the IRS and satisfied all thirty-two liens in two states.

WOLTA'II

Chapter 12

Mind over Matter

During this time, my parents attained a tribal ranch permit for grazing cattle. Even though they were in their eighties, the spirit of operating a cattle business never left them. During one meeting with the Grazing Committee, a question was asked to my parents, "Aren't you too old to be granted a permit?"

My mother responded, "I am not the one that's going to be chewing the grass, and I have strong young boys." So I became involved in the task of running a cattle ranch.

I enjoyed being around animals, so it was a labor of love. At one time, I was tracking down the ranch horses pulling a four-horse trailer when the trailer popped off the trailer hitch and broke the trailer jack. I looked around for something that I could use to prop the trailer high enough to reattach the trailer to the truck. It was useless since I was at a sandy location with no trees. I shoveled sand from under the rear tires of the truck to lower the hitch, but I still needed a couple of inches to join the hitches. Finally, it was obvious that the sun was setting, and if I was going to achieve something out of nothing, I had to do it with grit.

I knelt down next to the trailer and gripped the frame; I made sure my back was straight, and I was lifting with my legs; I gave a big howl; and with the inner core of my being, I summoned a burst of energy that was enough to lift the trailer onto the truck hitch. I could feel the bliss of my feat drain through my legs as I began driving the five hours to get home. When I arrived home, I opened the door, but I couldn't move; my body was locked in position. I tried moving my legs, but all I could do was wiggle my toes. I honked the horn of the truck, and my two big boys, Jay and Gil, stepped out of the house and asked, "What's up?"

I said, "I can't move!" They laughed, thinking I was pulling a prank on them, but once they knew I was serious, they pulled me from the truck. I asked if they could fill the tub full of hot water, thinking that it might loosen the muscles. They dipped me into the tub with my clothes still on. It barely relived the muscles. Then a sharp pain shot down my left leg that was excruciating. There was no relief from the pain no matter how I positioned my legs, so I stood motionless. I finally asked that they take me to the hospital.

For the next week, I was examined and reexamined by numerous physicians, and finally a decision was reached. I had herniated a disc in my lower back, and my vertebra was compressed causing the soft tissue to spread out, making contact with my nerves. According to the doctors, my best option to relieve the pain was for me to get surgery. The doctors explained that they would cut out the tissues that were touching the nerves. However, if they accidently slipped and happen to cut the nerves, I would be paralyzed from the waist down. Even if the surgery was a success, I would not be able to ride a horse, run, or play golf or any sports that required quick reflexes, which covers all of the above. As agonizing as the pain was, thinking of spending the rest of my days in a wheelchair would be unbearable.

I decided against the surgery, and I opted for alternative treatment. For the next year, I went to chiropractors, mud doctors, acupuncture treatments, electrical stimulations, medicine man, and salt water treatment. None was successful in eliminating the pain. It still took me fifteen minutes to cross the kitchen floor, doing the Texas two-step. Finally, I had enough treatments, but I was tired of being in pain.

I used to run or jog three miles each morning. Accordingly, one morning, I pulled my sweat pants on with a lot of effort. I put on my running shoes and slowly laced my left side up. I pulled my hooded sweat jacket on, and I scooted out the door. I took aim at my first distance, which was a cedar tree north of the house. It was about 150 feet away. I took one step then another, ignoring the pain. I reached about half way, and I was sweating and tired. I turned around and headed back toward the door, imagining that I was sprinting. I made it back to the door exhausted, but pleased. The next day, I repeated the same routine. It took a week to reach the cedar tree. The pain didn't go away; it was a constant reminder of the hurdle I had to overcome with each step. My next goal was to reach the corner of the driveway, double the distance of the cedar tree. I established a routine. When I rose out of bed, I would stretch as if I was going to run a marathon. Then

I perceived myself actual running, feeling the wind in my face, and gasping for air to fill my lungs as I began putting on my running gear. I reached the corner in two weeks. I was pleased with my progress, but when the excitement wore off, I was still struggling with my movements. Next, when I turned the corner, my goal was to reach the frontage road in front of the house, approximately 300 yards. It was a challenging target. I had many struggles, but I kept the routine and rehoned my imagination so I could focus on the details. I saw almost every pebble as I stepped over them. I carried a bottle of water to quench my thirst with each step. After one month, I arrived at the frontage road! I wasn't done. I had a new feature to reach, a two-lane highway a half a mile north of the house. By now, I had confidence and energy that I could do it. In my mind, I put the pain in my legs as a secondary nuisance. I focused more on the details of the inspiration of actually running. The process blurred between reality and conception.

All of a sudden, one morning, I began running! I thought, *Am I really running, or is it my imagination?* I looked at my shadow, and my legs were moving without pain! I reached out and touched the grass as it brushed against my hands. I moved my arms like a sprinter without any pain. I reached the highway in two minutes. I made a U-turn and began running home with a smile, ear to ear. The breeze that I had visualized was no longer a dream. I was truly feeling the airstream in my face. When I ran past the cedar tree, my kids were on the front lawn stunned with disbelief.

In their expressions of concern, they said, "You're not supposed to be running."

I thought, *Exactly*, but I didn't accept that assessment. Nor did I let it influence my actions, even though the pain validated their judgment. I have never received any treatment on my back to this day. The sciatic nerve fires off a sting now and then when I make awkward movement or lift a heavy object. But in general, I can ride a horse, play a round of golf, or run a half a marathon without issues. When the thought crosses my mind, *Did I really have this experience?* all I have to do is touch my lower spine and locate the vertebrae protruding out to verify that this incident indeed happened. I believe we all are born with an auto-repair system built inside of us. We just have to engage it through our mind's eye. For instance, the next time you get a muscle cramp, do this. When your body warns you that you're getting a muscle cramp, muster the feeling of relief when the cramp subsides, and send that feeling from your mind to the area of the muscle cramp with conviction. Even though you are contradicting the transmission from your muscle during the pain of the cramp, the body will accommodate your message, if it is delivered without doubt. As a consequence, your muscle cramp will recede as you continue to send the gratifying feeling of relief. However, if you fail to gather the feeling of relief absolutely, you will not stop the cramp.

This knowledge of discovering our potential to heal ourselves is the tip of the iceberg as human beings. Many studies have been done in this field through the ages by wise men, and many religious sects have admitted the power of faith. It is up to each of us to extend our awareness into the possibilities of medicinal healing.

Chapter 13

Return to My Craft

I returned to my trade in 2000 as a steamfitter welder. The transition from being an entrepreneurial to a construction worker was a tough one—mainly mental conflicts. I was used to calling the shots and in control of the charge; now I was relegated to grunt work, taking orders from supervisors that seemed to lack integrity and knowledge of the work. I was used to eating at fine tables; now I was taking boloney sandwiches in a lunch bucket to work and eating on steel structures. I used to walk into any car lot and buy whatever was in the showcase; now I couldn't finance a used car from a fraudulent dealership. At times, I flew in Learjets to get me to business meetings quickly, and now I had to sign the "out-of-work list" at the union halls.

The majority of my work was on power plants that would shut down for a brief period to do maintenance. It was a demanding schedule, twelve-hour shifts, seven days a week until the outage was completed. It was dangerous work. Working on nuclear power plants always had the possibilities of being exposed to radiation. Safety was a priority. Those sites required extensive ten-year background checks. In addition, the security was significant. However, the friends that I made there were worth the trouble.

In order to gain employment, it meant that I had to be on the road the majority of the year, which put a considerable burden on my wife to raise the children in my absences. She was stern and demanding, taking no prisoners and no democratic form of government in our home. It was a dictatorial regime. As a result, the children received good grades, graduated from high school, and began attending colleges.

Chapter 14

Olympics

In 2001, we had three children in college. All were full of energy and spontaneous in various activities. They notified us parents that they had signed up to be participants in the 2002 opening ceremonies of the Winter Olympics in Salt Lake City, Utah. They wanted to know if we wanted to join them. Since there were limited spaces available, we had to decide quickly. I declined the offer because I am not a dancer, but my wife accepted and was enrolled as one of the fortunate participants from the Navajo Nation as a dancer. Over the next few months, there were several rehearsals. Unfortunately, she missed one of the rehearsals due to schedule conflicts. She was relegated to an alternate to her disappointment. In December of 2001, the final selections were being made for those who were going to participate, during the same day that my foster father was being honored by the town of Spanish Fork for turning eighty years old. He called me and asked if I could attend the banquet. I said I would be there and nothing could keep from being in attendance, little did I know that my life would be altered in a different direction.

We arrived in Salt Lake City early. My wife went to the auditorium, hoping that she may be chosen in the final selection, even though her chances were slim. I, my brother-in-law, and his girlfriend followed a few hours later. We agreed that if my wife did not get picked, that we would all go to my foster father's banquet.

We located the building where the selection process was being made. However, the security was extremely tight due to the recent bombing of the Twin Towers in New York. There was only one entrance, and we had to show our identification to be permitted into the building. There was a young college-age Native American gentleman sitting at the front desk, and I observed his manner as individuals were asking to be admitted into the auditorium. No one was getting past his fortification. He seemed to almost take delight in turning away seekers. I turned to my brother-in-law and his girlfriend and said, "Let me do all the talking." I approached the young man, and without hesitation, I declared, "We're here!"

He was a little taken back and asked, "Who are you?"

I replied, "We are the singers that you requested."

He responded by saying, "I didn't ask for any singers."

I countered by saying. "We didn't travel twelve hours just to be turned back at this desk." He then explained that he had names of over a thousand individuals that were on the waiting list and that our names were not on the list. I repeated my statement, "We are not turning back after driving all night."

He continued by saying, "Even if I were to handwrite your names on the list, the chance of you getting selected is zero."

I then answered back, "Go ahead and put our names down."

He reacted and said, "I will write your names down, but don't even think of being selected."

I said, "Fine!" Mission accomplished! I had a giddy smile as we walked down the hallway, as if I just won a poker hand.

We found my wife waiting patiently in a cozy chair, and we sat next to her. I knew she very much wanted to be a participant. I respectfully said, "We can wait for another half hour, but we gotta go after that, so we won't be late for the banquet." She agreed.

Soon afterward, a lady wearing an Olympic jacket ran down the aisles to the front and in a desperate plea uttered, "Does anyone know how to handle horses?" My wife jabbed me in the ribs and urged me to raise my hand. I shook my head to say, "Nope," even though that's all I have done my entire life. My wife then tried a different approach. She said, "What if there's a horse that's loose and it might run over a little kid?" Well the guilt trip worked. I raised my hand, and the lady motioned me to come quickly up the aisles and into a waiting van that shuttled people to the Olympic stadium.

I got dropped off in front of the stadium and was instructed to sit tight. I looked around for horses, but none were in sight. Instead, the place looked like a scene from a movie set; it was a busy site. There were people walking around in costumes from the old west pulling handcarts, and there were folks dressed in gold feathers. I was baffled at all the commotion. Then a lady walked over to me. She was carrying a large phone. She said, "You are a very important part of this whole deal." Then she asked if I knew anyone else that can handle horses.

I said, "Yeah, my brother-in-law."

She asked, "Where is he?"

I responded, "The same place I was at a few minutes ago." She called the auditorium and requested him by name. My brother-in-law doesn't really know how to handle horses, but he is a big man. I figured all he had to do was lay down if he ever got in trouble. No horse could drag him too far.

A few minutes later, my brother-in-law was dropped off by the same shuttle. He walked over to me and asked, "What's up?"

I said, "I don't know, but we're a big deal." We watched the activity of different groups getting organized. The electricity was already in the air. I observed the lady with the big radio on her hip as she would redirect lost individuals while talking to someone on the radio. She made her way to us and explained that we were the "wranglers." She turned to me and pronounced that I was the head wrangler. She further clarified that there were five Native tribes in Utah, the Navajos, Paiutes, Shoshonis, Goshutes, and Utes. These were the tribes that would participate in the opening ceremony. Each would provide a spiritual leader that would enter the stadium on horseback. The wranglers would lead the horses onto the platform and down onto the ice, stopping at the anterior stage. There the spiritual leaders would dismount and walk onto the platform and welcome the 2,399 athletes and seventy-eight nations to Utah for the XIX Olympic Winter Games. She stated that we would be considered VIPs, and there would be a place for us to eat and lounge in between rehearsals. She asked us if we had any questions.

My mind was already spinning, and I said, "I don't know if I can do this."

She quickly responded, "You have to!" I explained that my wife was an alternate and if she didn't get picked to dance, I would be unable to carry out my role. She asked, "What's her name?" I told her. Then she dialed the auditorium. I interrupted by uttering "his girlfriend too!" as I pointed at my brother in-law. Needless to say, my wife's dream of participating in the opening ceremonies came true.

With new opportunities, it does not often come free, not always in monetary values, sometimes in time management. To my dismay, I called my foster mother to inform her that I would not be able to attend my foster father's banquet. I could tell in her voice that she was disappointed. She asked, "Where are you?"

I answered, "I'm at the Olympic stadium." I waited for a sign of approval from her, but there was nothing but silence. If I could at that moment, I wished I could be in two places at the same time; in my mind I was.

My brother in-law and I spent time in the VIP tent before deciding to check on the kids and the women folks. They were housed in a massive tent that held all the tribes and other participants. The accommodations were sparse due to the sizeable crowds. As I was moseying near the fence that separated us from the family, one of my daughters, who was an excellent dancer and who had her own island platform, saw me. She firmly bombarded me with questions, "What are you doing here?" "You're not supposed to be here" "How did you get over there?"

I responded confidently, "I'm a big deal," then asked, "Are you hungry?"

She said, "All we have is hot chocolate."

I told her, "I'll be right back." With my brother-in-law's help, we fed the family through the fence with the food from the VIP feast table.

That evening, we had our first Native American rehearsal when the temperature dropped in the teens. I wasn't dressed for the conditions, but the energy that was in the stadium warmed up all those who participated in the festivities. I followed my script as a wrangler, noticing the horse was very well-behaved, and I connected with him naturally. He enjoyed the spotlight. We were given special spikes that slipped over our shoes so that we would not slide on the mirror ice. The horse also had the same type of grip on his shoes. The rider on the horse was a Ute spiritual leader, Clifford Duncan, a reserved elderly man. I could sense that he had a lot of wisdom behind his eyes. His every motion had an essence of purpose. He rode in the saddle without the regalia during the rehearsals.

I need to explain the difference between a regalia and a costume. A costume is something that clowns wear. Regalia is what the Native Americans wear as part of their culture and traditions. The main difference is that a costume has no real significance other than to give entertainment, while regalia, on the other hand, has value and worth. It requires significance and insight for every article of the wardrobe to bear. It is worn in high esteem.

Having reached the north end of the platform, I led the horse and rider onto the ice without any issues. The movements were made in rhythm and in unison. As I made my way to the center of the arena, the other four tribes joined in as we proceeded toward the south end of the stage. I noticed my daughter who was the highlight dancer. She is very talented, where she danced on an island. She was the one who questioned me on why I was there. She looked at me, and she stopped dancing. Her jaw opened as I waved at her while sporting a cynical grin. We reached the podium where the spiritual leaders dismounted onto a rubber mat, making it easier for them to walk onto the stage. We then led our horses out of the stadium. We had plenty of help from volunteers. We handed the reins to the owners of the horses who were very proud of their mounts, as they should be. I then raced up to the stadium seats and soaked in all the energy that stemmed from the singing and dancing on the platform and ice. The electricity in the air was stimulating and exciting. I realized how powerful individuals can become when they unite for a cause they believe in.

Over the next couple of months, we had several rehearsals. There were challenges for the five tribes of Utah to overcome and then merge as one. From the outside world, some do not realize that each tribe is totally separate in language, prayers, songs, dress, traditional food, homes, beliefs, and customs.

Some of the issues, behind the scenes on the road to the opening ceremonies, that I will share with you were as follows.

The Olympic committee requested that the tribes use rubber weapons instead of the real arms. The committee's position was that the television audience would not be able to know the difference. That was unacceptable to the tribes and became a nonissue.

The songs that were sung and performed in the performance were finalized after some haggling between tribes as each contended that the songs were not in their language and they could not dance to them.

The tribes had some issues as each spiritual leader would bless the stadium in their ritual way. Then another tribe would bless the stadium over the other's consecration. Eventually each tribe found a place of sacred sanctioning.

There were moments of humor as well. On one rehearsal night, it was bitter cold. A stand in Navajo spiritual leader was welcoming the nation of the world. He went off script and started rambling about how cold it was and that he wished that we could all just go home. The supersize television screen translated his message as eloquent as it was written, and he received a round of applause from the spectators attending, while most of the Navajos were amused and had a chuckle.

The president of the International Olympic Committee Jacques Jean Marie Rogge flew in from Europe just to watch the rehearsal of the Native American opening performance.

Afterward, he spoke to the tribes and thanked them for their participation. It was the first time in the history of the Olympic opening ceremonies that Native Americans participated.

One evening prior to one of the rehearsals, a battle of the bands broke out in the enormous tent that housed most all the participants. One tribe would sing with their drums; then another would try to outperform with volume in drums and cries. This went on unrelentingly as no tribe wanted to show weakness by reducing the level of uproar. You could feel the tension and friction in the tent, when out of nowhere, there came a quiet gentle sound as if a feather was floating down from the ceiling. Everyone took note and looked perplexed, trying to locate where this thin razor-sharp music was stemming from. The drumming stopped, and no one moved. Slowly the crowd shuffled to get a better place to listen. The music was soothing. It replaced the conflict with harmony and instilled calmness. Finally, it was revealed that the music was coming from the next tent. The performers were the Mormon Tabernacle Choir.

I had my own challenges. While I was helping my brother-in-law prepare his regalia, I cut myself with a knife that sliced deep into my finger. I notified a volunteer who almost fainted when I exposed the cut and blood squirted out. She alerted the medics, and I was transported by a golf cart to the elevators. We arrived near the top floor to the box suites that were turned into an emergency room with all the equipment, machines, and staff to care for a large number of casualties in case of a terrorist attack.

Fortunately for me, it was just a knife wound that required only a few stitches.

Finally, February 8, 2002, arrived for the opening ceremonies. Officially it was called the XIX Olympic Winter Games and commonly known as Salt Lake 2002. The following is the relevant information: motto: Light the Fire Within, opened by President George W. Bush; cauldron: Members of the 1980 US Olympic hockey team, led by team captain Mike Eruzione; and stadium: Rice-Eccles Stadium.

We parked about twenty miles west of the stadium and were bussed to the onsite tents. The atmosphere was electrifying. It seemed like the participants were just floating on air. Everyone had a nervous smile. As we donned our regalia for the last time, we tried to relish every moment. We knew that we were accomplishing a part of history. One of the final preparations for male participants was to paint their faces with symbols that reflected the experiences and tradition of each tribe. The paintings were concealed until the last minute, and each man wore their image proudly, as if they were going into battle. My daughter painted the United States flag on my face, which I thought was appropriate for the event.

The security was extremely fortified as we made our way to the stadium. Uniform soldiers were screening those who entered the venue. FaceTrac System scanned every spectator entering the stadium as well. Jet fighters flew overhead, making continuous combat air patrol. All major airports were shut down during opening and closing ceremonies. Hazardous material crews were under the concourse ready to respond. The FBI and Secret Service had significant presence. An Elite Rangers Patrol secured the woods and mountains around the Olympic venues.

The time had come to execute what we had rehearsed. We all took our positions around the stadium. I was located at the main entry at the south end with my spiritual leader who was already on the horse. He looked magnificent with his headdress and staff. The festivities began by US President George W. Bush declaring the opening of the 2002 Winter Games. The Mormon Tabernacle Choir sang the national anthem.

Our time was nearing when the athletes began lining up to enter the stadium. Two thousand three hundred and ninety-ninety (2,399) athletes from seventy-eight (78) nations were present. We were told not to interfere with them. Barrier tapes were placed to keep the aisles clear for the athletes to march in. When the first of the seventy-eight (78) nations was introduced, one of the members came over and asked if it would be okay to get a photo with us. I said it was okay with us as long as we were not interfering with them. They jumped over the barrier tape and quickly posed as a team with us, then ran back in line. Then the next nation followed the same succession, soon all the nations were posing with us prior to entering the stadium. The barrier tape was trampled down and discarded. Unfortunately, I never obtained copies of the photographs because I didn't carry a phone.

Finally, the signal for me to lead the Ute Spiritual Leader had arrived. The lights in the stadium were blacked out. The sound of flutes came from all four directions. A golden eagle was released from the top of the venue and began descending in a circular pattern. That was my cue to enter and begin leading the horse down the platform. I had the trust of the horse and rider as we made our way in the dark. Suddenly, the spotlight hit us! You could hear seventy-two thousand (72,000) spectators breathe out in unison, a sigh of striking approval. Outside the stadium, the Olympics captured roughly half of the planet's attention, an estimated 3.5 billion people tuned in.

Never in the Native American history has there been a moment in time where we had the opportunity to showcase ourselves to the inhabitants of the planet. For the next thirty minutes, we sent a message that we are not extinct like the dinosaurs, but are complete and blossoming as a rose. We shared ourselves through our songs and our dances. We dressed in our regalia, and we spoke our native languages when we welcomed all tribes of man to our land. We asked that each nation respect one another through good sportsmanship.

As I reached the end of the platform, I led the horse and rider onto the ice for the last time. I finally was able to see the magnitude of the spectators in the arena. I felt so humble to represent myself, my family, my tribe, and my nation. I knew I was a part of history that would stand the test of time. The energy from the songs and the dancing seemed to move me forward without touching the ice. When we reached the platform, the spiritual leaders dismounted and began walking up the stairs onto the stage. We the wranglers exited the incredible ambiance that vibrated within the membrane of the Olympic stadium.

I realized that I had just performed a feat that only a handful of human beings would ever experience. I was fortunate enough to be given the opportunity to be a wrangler in the opening ceremonies of the Winter Olympics. It truly was a miracle.

I believe we are all given opportunities in life to expand our capabilities. On occasions, we grasp onto those chances, and at times, we fail to take advantages of those openings. Therefore, when extraordinary opportunities arise, we must become extraordinary to meet the requirements. Hence, when we do come out of our comfort zone and take action, we are rewarded tenfold. Some probabilities only come to us once in our lifetime. If we are not prepared, then we forfeit that experience. However, some prospects keep coming into view over and over until we take action. Everything in the making is ahead of you, not behind you. Don't let your personal history disintegrate new visions.

My family members that participated in the opening ceremony regrouped at the motel afterward. We already were going through the aftermath of our involvement. A quiet tone of calmness filled the room. Each person seemed to replay their experiences and ask, "Did we really take part?" Then the stillness was interrupted when someone turned on the television and a news channel was rebroadcasting the opening ceremony. The excitement resurfaced, and the energy once again became contagious. We celebrated into the twilight with pizzas and sodas.

The next day, my wife and I took the train to the Olympic Village to exchange pins and buy souvenirs. We stopped at the tent where we congregated as the Native participants and found some members of the Ute Nation gathering up their personal belongings. One of the Ute tribal members motioned me over and presented me with a full-body-length, hooded red ski jacket with the emblem of the Ute Nation embroidered on the back; in the front was an engraving that read, "Olympic Participant." Those in attendance gave me a gratifying applause. After returning from our excursion to the Olympic village, our son asked if we had seen the newspaper. We answered that we hadn't. He gave me a copy of the Olympic edition of the *Daily Herald*, dated February 9, 2001, with the headline SPECTACULAR! I unfolded the paper and, to my surprise, saw a photograph of me and the Ute spiritual leader on the front page of the associated press. Today that print is on display in a building at Park City, Utah, where mementos from the XIX Olympic Winter Games are on exhibition. We have been cemented on record as Native American participants of the opening ceremonies of the Salt Lake 2002. Today, twenty years have passed, in my mind I relive that event from time to time as if it occurred yesterday.

Jerry F. Nez Hushkachin in green regalia,
Ute spiritual leader on the horse

Jerry F. Nez Hushkachin and Ute Spiritual Leader.

Jerry F Nez Hushkachin and Ute spiritual leader
on the tarmac, dancers in the background

Chapter 15

Health

Shortly after returning home and getting reestablished with our mundane daily duties of work for me and school for my wife, we noticed small bruise marks on her body. We went to the doctors who referred us to a specialist at the Banner-University Medical Center Tucson, Arizona. There they took multiple blood test and determined the cause of the bruises was aplastic anemia. It's a rare but serious blood disorder. The bone marrow, which is the soft tissue in the center of bones responsible for producing blood cells and platelets, wasn't making enough new blood cells. There was damage to the stem cells inside her bone marrow. Her symptoms included fatigue, weakness, dizziness, easy bruising, and bleeding. For the next two years, we made numerous trips for physical exams and blood test to check for low numbers of cells in her bone marrow. Her doctor created a treatment plan that included weekly blood transfusion and platelets infusions.

At first, the treatments were managing the illness, but as the months passed, the medication became ineffective. A second option was considered, using horse serum or horse antithymocyte globulin, but she was allergic to the serum, so a rabbit serum albumin was applied and that had positive results.

Her health had declined to a point that she and her eighty-five-year-old mother were in similar physical condition. It was difficult to perceive that only a year ago, she was running marathons and now she had difficulty stepping onto sidewalks. As members of the Church of Jesus Christ of Latter-day Saints, we continued to fast and pray vigilantly as family, friends, and community of Snowflake, Arizona. Even though she was suffering from the symptoms of the afflictions, she nonetheless had hope and would force a smile to reassure us all that she was okay.

The second treatment with the rabbit serum failed. We were running out of options and time. The final alternative was a bone marrow transplant. This is a procedure that infuses healthy blood-forming stem cells into her body to replace bone marrow that's not producing enough healthy blood cells. It is also called a stem cell transplant.

We were referred to the Mayo Clinic at the North Phoenix Campus. We were introduced to multiple teams of specialist. The obstacle that we faced was getting a matching donor. It is especially challenging among Native Americans because of the perception that it is unethical to donate any of your organs. The Mayo Clinic implemented a nationwide search for a matching donor.

During this time, my wife had many physical adversities, as well as mental hardships. On occasions, we would rush her to the emergency unit to have the doctors cauterize the nose bleeds that she would get from sneezing.

Some weeks, we were unable to get transfusion or infusion of platelets due to not having any donors. When occurred, she basically had to stay in a recliner to eliminate any accidents that would cause internal bleeding. I recall one day she was visiting her mother in Window Rock, Arizona, the capital of the Navajo Nation, when her nose began to bleed. She went to the local Indian Hospital. They were unable to treat her, as they had no available platelets. The hospital flew her to Phoenix Banner Hospital on a jet. Banner Hospital cauterized her nose bleed and infused platelets into her, discharging her the same day. The one-way flight lasted forty-five minutes. We received a bill four weeks later for nearly $100,000.

The doctors at Mayo Clinic advised my wife and me to get our house in order for we were running out of time to find a donor and things didn't look promising. At this time, my wife pleaded with the Lord, "If I must leave this world, take me when I am asleep." When you deliver all you are physically capable of, then you embody the mental and spiritual realm to continue enduring life. You weave in and out of consciousness when the physical pain becomes unbearable. It is as if the Lord gave us an extra gear to be present while we prevail or yield the fight.

Within days following the doctor's advisement of getting our house in order, we received word, from the same doctors, that a donor had been obtained! We were elated, but the strenuous process was just starting. Weeks of pain-staking preparations were taken to confirm the match. Numerous teams of doctors were busy evaluating and reevaluating every option. There was no room for inaccuracies. They had only one attempt. With time expiring due to my wife's health deteriorating, my wife agreed to have the bone marrow transplant even though the match turned out to be an eight-out-of-ten ratio or 80 percent identical pair. The possible success outweighed the possible end result.

After completing the pretransplant tests and procedures, my wife began the process known as the conditioning where she underwent chemotherapy. Some of the side effects were hair loss, fatigue, and nausea, just to mention a few. Afterward, it was time for her "rebirth" or transplant. The stem cells were infused into her body through a central line. We waited as the new cells traveled through her blood to her bone marrow. They multiplied and began making new healthy blood cells over the coming weeks. This is called the engraftment.

We stayed at the Mayo Clinic for ninety days where she was under close medical care. A friend of mine offered his house while we waited for a small studio apartment within five minutes of the hospital for another three months.

Her posttransplant recovery treatments required numerous medications. Some concerns included her immune system, diet, and lifestyle. It takes time for the immune system to recover, so she received medication to prevent infections, prevent graft-versus-host disease (GVHD), and reduce her immune system's reaction. We had a team of dietitian's suggestions to help control side effects of chemo, plus guidelines to prevent foodborne infections, and a list of a wide variety of healthy foods.

At the time of this writing, it has been three years and nine months since the transplant. Many miracles have happened with my wife's health as well as spiritual growth. Her blood type went from A positive to O positive. She is running again. In fact, she has signed up to run in Honolulu in December 2022. With support of our family, friends, and community, we have confronted a monumental hardship for five years and prevailed. It is a testimony that if enough individuals come together for a common cause, then we can sway the outcome to our advantages.

The human body is made up of trillions of cells, each with its own structure and functions. The average membrane potential according to Bruce H. Lipton, Ph.D., is 70 millivolts or .07 volts. If there are 50 trillion cells X .07 volts = 3.5 trillion volts! Consequently, we each have the potential power that can be effective for healing or destruction.

When things look bleak and desperate, these are the times you have to look at things in a microscope and find any positive traces of promises of healing. One little spark of hope can start an inferno of restoration.

Life is like running down a hallway, and all of a sudden, you run into a six-foot wall of Jell-O. It feels like you're going to die. It takes your breath away, and you can't move. Slowly you begin to fight and begin inching your way forward. It takes will power and faith to not give up. Eventually, you will struggle through this barrier, you will gain your balance, you can take a deep breath, and you can relax before you start running down the hallway of life again. That is until you hit another six-foot wall of Jell-O.

After ninety days in the hospital and three months near the facility, my wife was given approval to return home. However, while we were busy with the medical treatments, we received word from our family that our house caught on fire. We lost 90 percent of the household items and personal belongings from smoke damage. We were placed in the local motel while the house was being restored.

No matter how crushing the news of the house fire was, it did not have the negative force to put us in a mental collapse. We realized through our experience that the fight for a human life versus the loss of material possession is significantly diverse. You can replace man-made substance; on the contrary, human life cannot be duplicated, therefore priceless. We were grateful that no one was hurt. In time, we restored the house and replaced the items that were destroyed.

WOLTA'II

Chapter 16

Summary

When we are born, we have no clue where we are globally, what sex we are, the color of our skin, nor the ethnic group we belong to. We cannot feed ourselves. We are naked, and we urinate on ourselves. We are helpless. So who are we? Why are we here? Where did we come from? And where are we exiting to?

We are spiritual beings having a brief human experience. We are here on a mission to learn and gain knowledge through living life on earth. When we were born, we came through a veil that purged our memory of where we came from. If not, it would hinder our enlightenment and our spiritual progression. As a result, what is our mission? The answer is the same and different for everyone, just as numerous as sand on a seashore. So is the number of souls that have lived on this earth, seeking to obtain and understand the answer to their mission. Each of us is born with talents. These gifts will assist us on a path leading to our purpose. Only you will know when you have fulfilled the quest. When our mission is complete, we will return from where we came by leaving our mortal body, similar to our hand slipping out of a glove. We do not die. Our mission continues.

During our time here on earth, we ponder many questions. We seek answers through many avenues. Each tribe of men have their own beliefs and ways of life. I remember trying to teach my Navajo family how the White man prays. But they would say, "That is the way of the White man. It is not meant for us."

Then, when I went to live with my foster family, I would explain how my Navajo family prayed. My foster father would say, "It's not the Christian way. It doesn't have the power of the priesthood." Yet, I saw that both ideologies were sacred and both prayers were answered. I realized that the force behind the power of prayer was in the belief that prayers will be answered, whether it was performed with corn pollen, cedar smoke, consecrated oil, holy water, eagle feathers or other means.

Some doctors experiment using sugar pills to cure illness, called the placebo effect. Because of the patient's belief that they will be healed, a strong connection between the brain and body is developed. Since we are spiritual beings, we have the ability to utilize the power of the heavens for healing, but for the reason that we are human, or natural man, we can also convert the energy into a negative force.

Understandings and gaining knowledge takes many years. Other species may take only one season to become fully grown and capable of taking care of themselves. Life expectancy, on average for man, is just above seventy years, which is insignificant compared to the eternal life of the universe. However, it is a very important time for our development. Our season here on earth is short. We must take advantage of each day to create a bit of heaven for ourselves. Everyone gets new twenty-four hours each day—young or old, female or male, rich or poor, etc. The questioned is, what are we going to do with the precious opportunity?

By coexisting as spiritual beings having a human presence, we have the capacity to function in both realms. In the spiritual state, we are one with all eternal fields. In the terrestrial existences, we are united with all things earthly. When I came out of my body, I saw myself standing in the kitchen. I could hear the water running from the faucet. Yet, I was not looking through my physical eyes, and I was not hearing with my carnal ears. I understood that I have bodily and spiritual features simultaneous cohabitating.

Having this form, we have been creating our own environment without any tutoring because of our natural ability to see with our mind's eye what we desire. Then we act upon those aspirations in the secular state. Inevitably those aspirations must come to pass if we put enough desire, belief, and force behind it. If you do not believe that you have selected your present state of being, just think back two years as a starting point and reverse engineer every choice that you made. It will lead you to where you are today. You are a powerful entity, fortified with all the means to accomplish your purpose for gaining a physical body. You cannot blame your misfortunes on the color of your skin, ethnic heritages, sex, age, and other metaphors with which we empower our limitations. If we are prudent in our aspirations, we must have harmony between the spiritual and physical field.

In my Navajo tradition, we enter the sweat lodge, which is a sacred structure for cleansing the mind and body. Other cultures practice meditation in different forms to achieve unity—attending the temples, monasteries, shrines, nature, etc.

When we reflect on human being's historical testament, we notice that we united as nations and erected splendid edifices on this planet, and we also see their departures by examining the same structures as they lay in ruins. If we reverse engineer their destructions, we understand an incredible intense energy was discharged, enough to obliterate human civilizations and displace the landscape.

What caused these terrible devastations is being studied today. I would offer a perception based on the opinion that we are spiritual beings having a brief human experience. If we simplify our issues to an individual scale, we find that we start having tribulations when we misplace our union with the universe and earth. We lose harmony and become unpredictable. In this erratic state, much damage can occur to our well-being. If we magnify this assessment to entire nations, then we can see the substantial harmful consequences.

The human family has delegated themselves as the stewards of planet earth because we can reason and communicate with one another locally and globally. We believe we are the most intelligent species in this sphere. We have invented many great tools to make life simpler. We have traveled to the moon and back. Yet, the more we acquire information, the more irresponsible we emerge. We have gone astray from being in harmony with things on earth and in the heavens. We are seeing and living the magnitudes of these failures daily. Each day, many souls return to spiritual form, and many souls emerge as a human body. However, the earth where they are to gain experiences is becoming a perilous place. Our children, grandchildren, and great grandchildren are being challenged substantially. What can we do to change the direction of the abolition of man? We have a little time but not enough to procrastinate.

We need to offset the negative energies by propelling positive forces into the atmosphere. This can be accomplished by doing small acts of kindness unconditionally worldwide each day. This light of love will displace the dark filth of hatred, greed, and jealousy. You don't need to be wealthy to give or be muscle-bound to lift a helping hand to a stranger. We do not need keys to unlock the vitalities of friendships. We must serve others outwardly to grow; we have to stop self-serving inwardly where we will wither. We all possess all the instruments, coupled with hope and beliefs to formulate a great day and a brighter tomorrow for all.

As I conclude my writing, I have one final thought that I desire to share with you. During the course of my life experiences, I have come to realize, understand, and accept that there is a supreme being that is presiding over all the millions of universes and the millions of stars in each universe. We currently occupy one star in our galaxy. On this blue planet that we call earth is our home away from home. It was conceived and formulated for us. Over millennia of time, it has gone through many transformations. It has accommodated many diversities of species. It is inconceivable that all these occurrences just happen without any prearranged schemes. All phenomena prior, present, and future have and will be done under the umbrella of God's authority.

Counting the many tribes of men that have lived on this planet, so are the names of the all-mighty God. Tongues cannot label him, nor can the handy works of men depict him. So how do we come to grasp the idea of a supreme life force? Since we are half-spiritual beings and half-human beings, we must quiet the natural man. There are many rituals man has conceived to access the entrance to the spiritual realm. If we believe what we do to connect is true, we act with genuineness. Then we will misplace the mortal man, and we start becoming aware of God. This spiritual voyage is like transforming into a champion; it is an arduous task to accomplish, but staying a champion is the most challenging trial. Being a holy person is like being a shaman or medicine man in my tribe. We live, think, and act like a spiritual being. Being one with all things, beauty above you, beauty below you, beauty behind you, beauty in front of you, it is finished in beauty. It is finished in beauty. It is finished in beauty. It is finished in beauty.

About the Author

Jerry F. Nez Sr. is a full-blooded Native American, born in the fall of 1953 on the Navajo Indian Reservation. At age six, he began attending a boarding school managed by the Bureau of Indian Affairs, where he acquired his birthdate. After completing third grade, he entered the Indian Placement Program offered by the Church of Jesus Christ of Latter-day Saints, where he was raised by a Christian family during the school year and returned to the reservation for the summer. He attended Utah Technical College before becoming a member of UA Local 469. After serving a five-year apprenticeship, he became a journeyman steamfitter welder. After ten years of working as a steamfitter, he became an entrepreneur despite not having any business schooling. He started operating and expanding Navajo Rent-a-Flik into seven businesses in Arizona and New Mexico. After fifteen years, he returned to his trade as a steamfitter in 2000.